CONSTRUCTING
THE CHILD

CONSTRUCTING THE CHILD

A History of Canadian Day Care

by Donna Varga

An Our Schools/Our Selves Title

James Lorimer & Company Ltd., Publishers
Toronto, 1997

For subscribers to *Our Schools/Our Selves: a magazine for Canadian education activists*, this is issue #50, the Second of Volume 8.

The subscription series Our Schools/Our Selves (ISSN 0840-7339) is published six times a year. Publication Mail Registration Number 8010. Mailed at Centre Ville, Montreal, Quebec.

Canadian Cataloguing in Publication Data

Varga, Donna 1959–
    Constructing the child: a history of Canadian day care

(Our schools/our selves, ISSN 0840–7339; no. 22)
Includes bibliographical references.
ISBN   1–55028–540–8

1. Child care – Canada – History. 2. Day care centers – Canada – History.
I. Title. II. Series.

HQ778.7.C3V37 1997   362.7'12'0971   C96–932505–3

Design and typesetting: Tobin MacIntosh.

Front Cover Design: Nancy Reid.

Our Schools/Our Selves production: Keren Brathwaite, David Clandfield, Lorna Erwin, John Huot, Doug Little, Magda Lewis, Bob Luker, George Martell, Brian Pastoor, Claire Polster, Satu Repo (Executive Editor), Bairu Sium, Harry Smaller.

James Lorimer & Company Ltd., Publishers
35 Britain Street
Toronto M5A 1R7

Printed and bound in Canada by La maîtresse d'école inc., Montreal, Quebec.

Contents

CONSTRUCTING THE CHILD

v

Tables

Figures

Photo Credits

Note: Materials cited in the footnotes as *newspaper article*, are unreferenced clippings located in the archival collections noted.

Acknowledgements

This book is the outcome of a long process of exploring, analyzing and writing, and I am indebted to many persons for their contributions. My thanks are extended to Philip Corrigan, for the important role he played in helping me realize the intellectual richness within our everyday working lives. Roger Simon, Bruce Curtis and David Livingstone were essential participants in the thesis version of this material.

Projects of this nature would be impossible if it were not for our guardians of history. Staff at the Provincial Archives of Manitoba, University of Toronto Rare Book Library, Metropolitan Toronto Reference Library (Baldwin Room), and the National Archives of Canada are gratefully acknowledged for their assistance.

Financial support was provided through small grants from the University of Saskatchewan Department of History, University of Manitoba Senate, and more substantially through a University of Saskatchewan new faculty grant.

Eleanor Cohen provided diligent research assistance. Susan Prentice initiated the book project. Lorna Erwin reviewed the manuscript. Satu Repo provided critical commentary and encouragement.

Earlier versions of some sections in the book were published in *Advances in Early Education and Day Care*, 1993.

Robert Lanning provided scholarly comradeship by subjecting himself to repeated readings, offering substantive reviews, and insisting that I believe in myself. Finally, the completion of this project despite the twists and turns of life is indebted to the inspiring strength of spirit and determination of my mother, Vicky Varga.

Chapter One

Introduction

In 1939, Helen Thomas was matron of the Mothers' Association Day Nursery, the first day nursery to be established in Winnipeg. Day nursery is the historical term for agencies whose essential purpose was to provide a place where children could be cared for during the day, while their parents worked or were otherwise unable to provide home care. In the contemporary period, these agencies are referred to as day care or child care centres. The children cared for by Mrs. Thomas were primarily of Eastern European origin or descent and were from families that were financially destitute. In these ways they reflected the ethnic, cultural, economic, and social status of the community in which the nursery was located. Mrs. Thomas had been matron of the nursery since 1925, and would remain in that position until 1942. In many ways she was similar to other day nursery matrons during the first half of the twentieth century; she was an older woman, probably widowed, and without any special training (her previous employment was as a binder at the *Winnipeg Saturday Post*). As matron, Mrs. Thomas was responsible for the day-to-day running of the nursery: she looked after the children who ranged in age from infancy to ten or twelve years, supervised the nurse who cared for the infants and youngest children, and oversaw the nursery's domestic staff. In addition, she managed the nursery's employment service.

If Mrs. Thomas were to return to her day nursery at the end of the twentieth century she would find that many things had changed. She would be informed that the role of matron no longer existed; that she could not hold a supervisory position unless she had special training in early childhood education; that the schedule on the wall laid out what activities children should be doing at particular times of the day; and that mothers no longer applied to the nursery in order to find work as domestics in the homes of the economically privileged. If Mrs. Thomas chatted with the nursery's current caregivers about how she used to care for children, they would probably consider her stories to be examples of the bad old days of child care. While she might agree that many aspects changed for the better, Mrs. Thomas might not be convinced that everything she saw was for the good of the child.

This book sets out to explore the history of ideas and practices of child care as carried out in Canadian day nurseries from their establishment in the late nineteenth century. Ideas about how children should be cared for in day nurseries were very different in the late twentieth century than those of the late nineteenth century. This book begins by looking at what care was like, and the beliefs about children that the care was based upon. The roles of the nurseries as social service agencies for mothers, the characteristics of good caregivers, and methods of child care are described from the 1890s. A primary emphasis of those practices was on providing for the physical well-being of children, with little interest paid to staff training, equipment, timetables or observation of children. These aspects of day nursery practices are often now criticized as evidence that the children received poor quality "custodial" care.[1] This book provides the context for those caregiving practices. In the period before 1920, the primary function of the nurseries was to enable mothers who were poor to engage in paid employment. This does not mean that the children were not cared for, or cared about. That the nurseries should provide a healthy environment for children was considered important, but prior to the mid-1920s, this meant a healthy physical environment. There was not yet a belief that children's social, emotional, or intellectual development needed to be supported by the nurseries.

Most histories of day nurseries explain changes in caregiving practices as an evolutionary accumulation of knowledge that has replaced poor care with good care.[2] Contrary to such interpretations is Steinfels' detailed history of U.S. day nurseries.[3] Steinfels identified the 1920s as a benchmark period. Since that time nursery school and social work professionals have been influential in changing caregiving practices in the day nurseries. While she acknowledges that nursery school professionals' "skills and influence undoubtedly raised the quality of child care," she also noted that their professional outlook resulted in "unfortunate" changes.[4] The major problematic change identified by Steinfels was the elimination of care for children under two or three years of age, leaving working mothers of younger children without nursery services. Steinfels explains this as an "unintended consequence" of the fact that nursery school teachers did not have knowledge of theories and methods for caring for the younger children, and from their focus on educational activities in which the younger children could not engage.[5]

In this book, changes to Canadian day nursery practices are explained somewhat differently. After discussing the early nursery practices, this study outlines how in Canada, the University of Toronto Institute of Child Study was central in the creation of a system of caregiving practices that I refer to as the normative curriculum. The Institute was established in 1925 (originally as the St. George's School for Child Study) just as child study was gaining credence as a science. The earlier investigations into childhood by G. Stanley Hall had spawned widespread interest of parents and teachers in understanding how children were different from adults. The 1920s research by Arnold Gesell into stages of children's development provided the basis for the research carried out at the Toronto Institute. In addition to scientific child study, ideas about mental health were crucial to the model of care provided at the Institute's nursery school. It was argued that young children needed to learn to adjust to social environments in order to become mentally healthy adults, and thus good citizens.

Having a centre for child study and a nursery school within a University was one thing, but having its practices transferred to day nursery care was another. After describing the history of the Toronto Institute and the normative curriculum of its nursery school, this book explains how the Institute became the major influence over caregiving practices in Canadian nurseries after 1925, through publications, membership in different organizations, public speaking and training activities, and through the establishment of Canada's first day nursery regulations.

The nurseries adopted the normative curriculum of the Institute's nursery school, and in doing so their primary concern for the needs of mothers was superceded by a concern for the developmental supervision and management of children. Children who could not be fitted into the new ideas of good care were no longer provided with nursery services. This meant an end to day nursery care for infants and school-age children. Even though not all the nurseries immediately embraced the new model of care, what did occur was a process whereby the normative curriculum became dominant. This explanation differs from the view that changes in nursery practices resulted from a natural and positive progression in knowledge and practice, or as a side-effect of personnel not prepared to care for particular children. Instead this book demonstrates that ideas and practices were purposefully reconstructed to correspond with new beliefs about the nature of the child. The incorporation of the curriculum of the Institute's nursery school into the day nurseries was more than a simple substitution of what by the 1940s was considered 'poor care,' for good care. Instead, there was a transformation in how caregivers' thought about children: their beliefs about children's development and what they considered to be the important emphasis in child care.

Ideas about the nature of the child underwent further changes in the 1960s in North America. The emphasis from that period was on cognitive development, especially as theorized by Jean Piaget, and on the intellectual development of infants. These theoretical developments occurred along with the campaign in the United States, and later in Canada, to eradicate poverty through early childhood education programs known as Head Start. Unlike the ideas about child development and child care that emerged in the 1920s, those of the 1960s did not transform the normative conceptual framework for understanding the child. Instead, the new emphases became integrated into the normative curriculum. The attitudinal changes created by the women's movement also meant that an increased number of mothers with preschool children entered the paid labour force. The resulting political pressures for child care led to an expansion of caregiving services. This included the reintroduction of nursery provisions for infants and school-age children, and the availability of day nursery care for children of the middle class. By the 1990s the dominant ideology and practice of the normative curriculum faced challenges of adequately serving the needs of an increasingly diverse population along with a lack of political commitment for publically supported child care.

By tracing the histories of Canadian day nurseries and linking their practices to ideologies about the child, this book reveals the roots of what has become commonsense knowledge about children's care. In doing so, the book challenges the interpretation of past practices as 'bad' and current practices as 'good,' and thereby attempts to stimulate critical discussion about early childhood care and its future direction.

FOOTNOTES

1 See for example Cahan, E. D. 1989. *Past Caring: A History of U.S. Preschool Care and Education for the Poor, 1820-1965*. NY: National Center for Children in Poverty; Schulz, P. 1978. "Day care in Canada: 1850-1962." In K. Gallagher Ross (Ed.), *Good Day Care: Fighting For It, Getting It, Keeping It*. Toronto: The Women's Press, pp. 137–221.

2 Cahan, 1989; Pence, A. 1987. "Child Care's Family Tree: Toward a History of the Child and Youth Care Profession in North America." *Child & Youth Care Quarterly, 16*:151–61; Schulz, 1978; Wrigley, J. 1990. "Children's Caregivers and Ideologies of Parental Inadequacy." In E.K. Abel & M. K. Nelson (Eds.), *Circles of Care: Work and Identity in Women's Lives*. NY: Albany: SUNY Press, pp. 290–312.

3 Steinfels, M. O'Brien. 1973. *Who's Minding the Children? The History and Politics of Day Care in America*. NY: Simon & Schuster.

4 Steinfels, 1973, p. 57.

5 Steinfels, 1974, p. 59.

Chapter Two

Day Nursery Child Care
Social Service Agencies For Mothers

It is its intention to enable *struggling and deserving women to help themselves*, by taking care of their children by the day, or the week, and by so doing make it easier for the parent to earn the necessary means of support for her family. This means to bathe, feed, teach and often to clothe the children; in many cases to give them medical treatment, and in *all cases* to give them a dentist's care. The Nursery also opens its doors as a *temporary* home to children whose mothers are ill, and for the time being in hospital, while in return for care given a small payment is expected, so that the help offered will not pauperize.[1]

In the late nineteenth and early twentieth centuries, Canadian day nurseries were established by religious and charitable agencies, and volunteer philanthropic upper class women, to care for the children of working mothers.[2] In this chapter, the description of early Canadian day nursery child care is carried out through a discussion of the policies and practices of six such institutions. This book does not provide a complete history of each of the nurseries, but draws on evidence available from each to provide a picture of day nursery care from the late 1800s. The official names of the nurseries are set out in Table 2.1. For convenience, they will be referred to by the following: East End Day Nursery (established in 1892, closed in 1959), West End Creche (established in 1909, limited its services to children with special needs from 1956), Victoria Day Nursery (established in 1890), Ottawa Day Nursery (established in 1911), Winnipeg Day Nursery (established in 1909), Montreal Day Nursery (established in 1888).

Table 2.1 Official Names of Day Nurseries

Victoria Day Nursery*
1890 — The Creche Nursing Institute for Children
1952 — Victoria Day Nursery
1967 — Victoria Day Care Services

East End Day Nursery
1892 — East End Day Nursery

West End Creche
1909 — West End Creche
1956 — Treatment Centre for Emotionally Disturbed Children

Montreal Day Nursery
1888 — The Day Nursery and Industrial School of Montreal
1900 — Montreal Day Nursery

Ottawa Day Nursery
1911 — Ottawa Day Nursery
1970 — Andrew Fleck Child Centre

Winnipeg Day Nursery
1909 — The Mothers' Association Day Nursery
1953 — Day Nursery Centre

* The names in capital letters are the names that will be used throughout this study in reference to the nurseries

A brief outline of the origins of some of the nurseries provides insight into the similarity and diversity amongst them. The Montreal Day Nursery was established in 1888, under the sponsorship of Reverend Dr. Barnes, and during its first summer of operation, became a branch of the YWCA. That organization provided the nursery with a house from which to carry out its services. In 1900 it became an independent agency and was reincorporated under the name Montreal Day Nursery.[3] The Ottawa Day Nursery was established in 1911 as part of that city's settlement house.[4] In 1916 it was reincorporated as a separate agency. The Victoria Day Nursery was organized in 1890, in response to the caregiving service being provided by Hester How, a teacher in a public school in one of Toronto's most financially destitute districts. Faced with the problem of poor school attendance because the children remained at home to care for their younger siblings, How permitted pupils to bring the infants to school. It is reported that while teaching, she provided care for the infants, "feeding them and laying them on benches to sleep."[5] This was apparently successful in increasing school attendance, but must have created great difficulties for Miss How, who had to care for babies as well as carry out her teaching duties. In 1890, James Hughes, Inspector of Education for Toronto, obtained a $50 yearly grant from the school board "for care of the little ones in a room at the Old Folks Home on Emma Street."[6]

The East End Day Nursery was established by members of

East End Day Nursery 1902–1903 Dining Room: Children ate in large groups at an adult sized table.

the Quaker Mission in Toronto, in 1892. It initially operated in the upper room of the Mission Sunday School house. The Winnipeg nursery was founded in 1909, by that city's Mother's Association, a group of wealthy women interested in philanthropic activities. The nursery was established as part of the Association's objective of engaging in "social science or community influence."[7] During this early period of day nursery history, the income for carrying on the work of the agencies was obtained primarily through fundraising activities. The organizers held social events that were patronized by the wealthy. These included dinners, teas, Christmas parties, and fancy-dress balls. One such event sponsored by the East End nursery in the early 1900s was a benefit auction of dolls manufactured to resemble famous personalities. Occasionally a sizeable individual donation would be received, such as the $100,000 provided by Sir William MacDonald to the Montreal Day Nursery in 1903.

Some fundraising events were intended to derive income from the general public, such as rummage sales and tag days (street solicitation of money whereby donors would be pinned with a paper tag). Some of the nursery organizers formed a day nursery club for supporters and charged a membership fee. In 1916 members of the Ottawa Day Nursery Club each gave $12.00 annually, while board members each gave $60.00.[8]

By the early 1920s most of the nurseries had joined their local chapter of Federation of Community Service. This charitable financial association was the precursor to the Community Chest, and later the United Way. The Federation held annual canvasses of the public on behalf of all member organizations, which then received a percentage of the total amount collected. This relieved individual members of the nursery boards from having to find financial support for the agencies. However, it also meant some loss of autonomy for the nurseries as they were restricted in the type of public fundraising they could carry out. It also meant they had to abide by the funding agency's requirements in order to receive financial support, particularly in terms of child care admission policies. Upon joining the Federation, the Ottawa nursery organizers asked its nursery club members to make donations to the Community Chest instead of paying a club fee. This was later thought to result in members losing "personal contact," with the nursery and a consequent decline in support.[9]

The smallest portion of income for the nurseries came from parent fees. The destitute financial situation of families meant that they could not afford to pay the full cost of the service received. Charges at the Montreal nursery were typical, ten cents a day for one child or fifteen cents for two children. It was thought that requiring parents to pay even a small fee would support parental dignity (they were not receiving charity) and ensure they were not, as put by the Montreal organizers, "absolved from their parental responsibilities."[10]

Social Roles

The quote at the beginning of this chapter elucidates the original primary function of the nurseries; providing charitable social aid to relieve family poverty. All the nurseries operated in the poorest districts of their cities, their purpose being the care of children whose mothers *had* to engage in paid labour in order for their families to survive. Most of the mothers were widows, or were deserted by their husbands, or had husbands who were ill or otherwise incapacitated; as well, the nurseries cared for children of motherless families. The social service role of the nurseries was carried out through the provision of an employment service for women, offering them positions as domestic workers in the homes of the economically privileged or in the laundry services. Women brought their children to the nurseries when they had employment, or when they wanted to be placed in an employment position by the agency. It does not appear that the nurseries limited their provision of care to children of mothers who obtained work through the employment agencies, but it seems that many women used both these services. The success of the nurseries, as determined by the numbers of children cared for daily (over 100 during peak periods) and their continuity of existence, indicates the need women had for such agencies in order to find both work and child care.

Day nursery services were originally restricted to children whose families suffered conditions of extreme poverty. This meant that the wages of the father alone could not support the family, and even with both parents working the family was

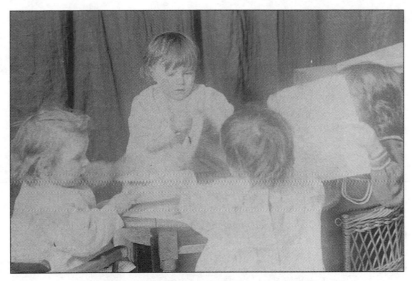

East End Day Nursery 1902–1903 "A Corner of the Nursery."

financially destitute. In order to receive the child care service, the mother had to prove to the nursery organizers that without her paid employment the family would be foodless and shelterless. Apart from the regulations requiring families to be living in conditions of poverty, the individual nurseries had more or less stringent rules about who should be accepted for the receipt of their services. The Montreal nursery seems to have been quite rigid, reporting vigilance in the 'type' of women who were to receive child care service. Its 1906 minutes provide an indication of the criteria women needed to meet if they were to be provided with nursery services:

> In some instances new women applied whose children were in a deplorable condition. They were taken to the Nursery for a few days, just long enough to be made clean and to be warmly clad, then the women left, never to return, or applied after a long absence and under another name, hoping that they had been forgotten and would receive the same help. Women of this class are not sent out to work from the nursery [and the children were not accepted into care].[11]

At the Ottawa nursery, until the 1960s, the women organizers made decisions about who would receive caregiving ser-

East End Day Nursery 1902–1903 "Where the Babies are Kept."
Children shared beds, and some slept while others played.

vices based on interviews with the mothers.[12]

In general, the admission of illegitimate children into care was determined on a case-by-case basis. A woman's first illegitimate child might be admitted, but if she had further illegitimate children, caregiving services would no longer be provided for her. While they were striving to prevent women from becoming social burdens, in order to maintain community financial support the nursery organizers could not be seen to be encouraging licentious behaviour. It is likely that some women claimed widowhood or desertion in order to bypass such negative sanctions.

All the nurseries were involved in a variety of charitable projects aimed at supporting the lives of needy families. Such activities included the organization of well-baby clinics,[13] dental and medical services, temporary residential homes for children, the distribution of food, clothing, and loans of money to the families they served. Other community services provided by the Ottawa nursery included looking after lost children, sometimes overnight, and providing free child care at the city's annual exhibitions.

Characteristics of Good Care

During the years of the late nineteenth and early twentieth centuries, good day nursery child care was that which supported the physical and moral well-being of the children. This was a time when all children, both those receiving nursery care and those cared for at home, were highly at risk of death from illness and disease. Of greatest threat to the children in the nurseries, particularly infants, were outbreaks of contagious diseases. Preschoolers and school-age children suffered mostly from measles, influenza, polio, mumps, whooping cough, scarlet fever, scabies, impetigo and chicken pox. The nurseries had, on occasion, to close down due to epidemics in the city, or because of the need to quarantine the nursery itself. In 1918, the Montreal Day Nursery stopped its nursery care and instead opened as an emergency clinic to help treat victims of the influenza epidemic. In 1922 it was closed because of an epidemic of scarlet fever and measles amongst its children. During that period, these diseases as well as diphtheria and gastritis took the lives of seven infants. The East End Day Nursery closed for two months in 1938 because of a city wide polio epidemic.

Health care of nursery children and often also of their families was provided through free medical and dental services, feeding of children, and supplemental milk for infants. From their earliest years the nurseries utilized the volunteer services of physicians and dentists so that the children would receive regular medical and dental examinations and treatments. That good care focused on physical health at the Ottawa nursery is indicated by its organizers' evaluation of the staff: "That the Nursery staff is an efficient one is evident from the clean bill of health for the year, no cases of infectious or contagious diseases having been reported."[14]

Beyond physical care, the concern of the nurseries during this period was the moral management of children while they attended the institutions. Some of the activities conducted along these lines included a Band of Hope organized by the Women's Committee Temperance Union, about 1900, to provide lessons at the East End Day Nursery, "with the object of teaching the children in the principles of temperance and proper living in the home."[15] It was reported that in 1911 "Canon Green has a little talk and Bible reading with the children on Wednesdays."[16] The Montreal nursery specified its caregiving tasks as being "to feed, to keep clean, to control, to instruct, to amuse, to keep out of mischief, and often to clothe."[17] At the Winnipeg nursery children were "instructed in the knowledge of Canadian customs, cleanliness and regularity."[18]

Severe punishment of children appears to have been frowned upon by some nursery organizers. The East End organizers decided, in 1916, that "a rule be put on the books that children must not be whipped in the Nursery."[19] Maizie Hill recalls that when children at the Ottawa nursery misbehaved the extent of punishment might have been a quick slap on the shoulder or a slight shaking.[20] In 1942 at this nursery the records report that "a teacher's qualification is such that she can handle her children properly without punishment of any kind."[21]

During this period, matrons and nurses were the primary caregivers. Matrons appear to have been older women, usually unmarried or widowed, with no special training in child care work. They often lived in the nursery buildings and oversaw daily operations including the supervision of the children, employment service, and housekeeping staff. The diversity of their tasks is apparent in a description of the Montreal nursery matron's work:

> The Matron's task has been a varied one. Besides the supervision of the house and its inmates, she has been called upon to settle all kinds of difficulties for the women, to visit them in their homes when they were ill, to send properly prepared food to sick babies, and to help with money from the Poor Fund, for funeral and other pressing expenses.[22]

The hectic pace of her job is further evident from a 1907 report: "during the busy months the calls for charwomen averaged thirty a day, and coming as they did at all hours, kept the matron from accomplishing her work."[23]

It is unclear whether the caregivers referred to as nurses had some health care training, or if the term was derived from 'wet-nurse.' In some cases, the former was true, such as for Elizabeth Anderson, Superintendent of the Ottawa nursery from 1916-1918, who had nursing training from the Royal

Alexander Hospital, Fergus Ontario. Nurses generally looked after the infants, carrying out such duties as preparing formulas, giving feedings, and administering medicines. Sometimes the matron and nurse were one and the same person, and in such cases their duties would have been even more strenuous.

A significant portion of the nurseries' staff consisted of housekeeping personnel such as maids, cooks and laundresses. Staff of the Montreal nursery, in 1890 included a matron, a nurse, an assistant nurse and a general servant.[24] In 1904 it included a matron, a teacher for the school age children, a cook, a laundress, nurses and nurse assistants.[25] It appears that the housekeeping personnel were involved directly in the care of the children and the caregiving staff also had to carry out custodial duties. At the Ottawa nursery for instance, the caregivers cleaned and sterilized the bathrooms and cleaned the nursery in general either when the children were sleeping or when the children went home at night.[26]

Occasionally, the staff was supplemented by school teach-

Mothers' Association [Winnipeg] Day Nursery (c. pre-1920s).
Children in sandbox with doll house.

Mothers' Association [Winnipeg] Day Nursery (c. pre-1920s). Outdoor playground.

ers, who provided lessons for the four and five year olds. These were usually short-term arrangements, dependent on voluntary teachers or financial support from a school board. In 1910, the West End Creche added a kindergarten teacher to its staff of matron, cook, nurse and housewife. She spent two hours on schooldays giving lessons "on sewing and deft use of fingers."[27] During 1917, a kindergarten was carried out at the Ottawa nursery for one hour each morning by an instructress who was paid by the school board. This ended after one year when she obtained employment at a public school and the School Board did not provide financially for a replacement.[28]

The small number of staff, the many physical needs of the young children, the often large numbers of children of different ages, and the multiple duties of staff made it unlikely that adults were able to devote a continuous length of time with individual or groups of children. A newspaper report on the Winnipeg nursery noted that "twenty-five babies, all under the age of four, is rather a large handful to manage — for three women."[29] Workers, therefore, moved continuously from one child to another, in order to carry out physical caretaking. The limited types of inter-actions between staff and children were described by the Mon-treal nursery matron, who, in 1904, stated that "much of her morning is taken up with dosing the weakly ones with cod liver oil and other tonics and attending to the numerous ear and nose ailments."[30] The busyness of the nursery day is illustrated by the comments made at the Ottawa nursery with regard to the 12,269 children cared for over the course of 1924-25:

> How many among that number received special attention has not been recorded. Those in charge are so busy looking after the welfare of the children that half a dozen more or less sick are expected and are all in a day's work.[31]

Maizie Hill recalled that caregiving work at the Ottawa nursery was tiring. Sometimes in the afternoons she would lie down with the infants in order to "have a sleep, because I'd be exhausted, running after them ... because there would be ten or fifteen of the under-two-year-olds running around." Maizie knew many of the Ottawa nursery staff quite well since she spent her childhood there, and because her mother had been that agency's cook for about 20 years. She remembers that the women worked six days a week for long hours, and after the children were gone "you had your own washing and cleaning up to do. I know that mother would have to go home then and clean our room where we lived." It was, Maizie believes, a hard life for the workers.

This form of adult-child interaction was not just a result of high child-staff ratios, but arose out of the prevalent ideas about children as competent beings. Maizie Hill remembered that when she was a child in the nursery, the children were responsible for creating their own entertainment. An adult was present and the children knew they could go to her if they needed help, but she did not direct the children's play. Inside the children had the use of a piano, puzzles, and books: "We would sit around and we would make up stories, and sort of entertained ourselves that way." She credits this for teaching herself and the other children "to use our minds ... you learned how to entertain yourselves." Her memories of staff interac-tions with the infants during the summer she assisted in the nursery also highlight the particular type of independence expected of children:

> When they came in, in the morning you changed them, put them in the nursery outfit. You sat them on the potty, you had to watch that they were diapered and you had to rush them to the potty if they needed one. You were just sort of there to watch over them, you had to be careful that they didn't hurt one another. They had things to play with, little building blocks, soft toys. The little ones were put into a play pen that fit into a corner of the nursery.

It is often assumed that in the early day nurseries, staff turnover was high, and that this demonstrated the nurseries' lack of quality child care. It is likely that the retention of child care staff varied amongst day nurseries, but as Table 2.2 shows, for the Ottawa and Winnipeg nurseries studied here, a number of women remained for many years. This was especially the case at the Ottawa nursery, where Clara Servage and Margaret Fleming worked for forty-five years each; where Susie O'Neill worked for at least forty-four years; where Lillian Batza worked for thirty years; and where Ruth Mentzell worked for twenty-two years. The fact that Servage, Fleming and O'Neill were related to each other may have influenced their decision to stay with the nursery for so many years. The long years of service by these three may also have resulted from the fact that up until the 1960s they lived in the nursery building, therefore being dependent upon this employment for their place of residence.

While it was the nurses, matrons, and housekeepers who carried out the day-to-day activities, they do not appear to have been responsible for decisions regarding child care policies. Such authority was retained by the women organizers. The voiceless role of the nursery staff is suggested by the following factors: the almost complete absence of reports by them; no mention of the staff in nursery minutes; no evidence that they attended nursery board meetings. At the East End Day Nursery, a Matron's report was included in its monthly meetings from 1903, but it consisted only of providing attendance figures and domestic needs, with no participation in regard to child care practices or policies.

Table 2.2 Day Nursery Employees

Selected Staff of the Ottawa Day Nursery

Name	Position	Years Of Service
Grace Mather	Convenor of Management	1916 - 1947
Margaret Fleming	Matron	1919 - 1964
Clara Servage	Caregiver	1920 - 1965
Susie O'Neill	Caregiver	at least 1924 - 1968
Emma Nelson	Director	1948 - 1950
Mary Leach	Caregiver	1948 - 1963
Mary Laing	Director	1950 - 1963
Lillian Batza	Caregiver	1949 - 1979
Ruth Mentzell	Caregiver	1956 - 1978

Selected Staff of the Winnipeg Day Nursery

Name	Position	Years Of Service
Mary J. Kyle	Matron	1917 - 1921
Helen Thomson	Matron	1925 - 1942
Margaret Merrifield	Nurse	1930 - 1952
Katherine Learned	Matron	1943 - 1952
Gretta Brown	Director	1953 - 1976
Mary L. Hughes	Social Worker	1954 - 1959
Barbara Rigby	Caregiver	1958 - 1985
Nettie Panting	Caregiver	1958 - 1968

Organization of Child Care

In their role as social service agencies, the nurseries' hours of operation were attuned to the long working days of the mothers.

Mothers needed the nurseries open from early in the morning until early evening so they could have time to travel to and from their work places by foot or horse-drawn streetcar. Most of the work the women did was housekeeping for economically privileged families, and the location of these homes was usually quite a dis-

Mothers' Association (Winnipeg) Day Nursery, 1939.
Mrs. Thompson, Matron, seated on stairs with children.

tance from the nurseries. The nurseries were open for eleven or twelve hours; from six or seven in the morning, to six or seven in the evening, Monday to Friday. The West End Creche and Ottawa Day Nursery were also open Saturday afternoons to care for children of parents who worked on that day. The Montreal Day Nursery regulated the arrival and departure of mothers to ensure that the needs of its employment service were met. The organizers stated, "The Committee have done their utmost to compel the women to enter their children at an early hour, so that they may give their employer a fair day's work, and for that reason no child is admitted after 8 a.m. The doors are open from 7 to 8 a.m., and from 5:30 to 7 p.m."[32] The rigour of the Montreal agency was not the practice of all the nurseries. At the East End, a more flexible schedule existed, with children being provided with care for full or partial days, allowing women to work part time hours, and possibly allowing them to determine their own hours of labour rather than having their workday defined by the nursery.[33] When the matron and nurse lived on the premises, they often provided care earlier and later than the official hours, sometimes even overnight. While this prolonged the labour of the caregivers, it was a solution to the child care problems faced by women who often had to travel a great distance to and from places of employment.

During the early years of the nurseries, the records provide few details about how their time was organized, and this lack of discussion might be evidence of it not being considered an important factor in the care of children. When the children arrived they were bathed and dressed in clean clothes or smocks. The children had at least two meals at the nurseries, a noon dinner and an evening supper. Between their arrival and meal time activities, the children played and slept as their interests and personal needs necessitated. At the Ottawa nursery the following schedule was described for 1925:

> When meal time comes around they are fed ... and when the tiniest of them rub their little eyes and show all the signs of needing a nap, nurse just picks them up and pops them into cosy beds on an upper floor where they sleep till thoroughly rested.[34]

At the Winnipeg nursery it was reported that the children spent some of their time cutting out pictures for scrapbooks, making paste and paper baskets.[35]

In their service to working mothers, the day nurseries provided care for infants of a few weeks old, preschoolers, and school age children. Ten years was probably the most common upper age of children, but in some cases, children of twelve or fourteen years were provided with care before and after school hours. Most children cared for were infants and under six years old. This provision of care for young children allowed women to work outside the home before the school could be utilized as a child care service. These families' needs for food, shelter and clothing could not wait for such a time, and the nurseries enabled at least some mothers of young children to engage in paid labour.

There were no day nursery policies or legal regulations governing such aspects as staff-child ratios or amount of space per child. Maximum numbers of children attending the nurseries were decided in terms of the number that the organizers thought could be accommodated within the building and looked after by the staff. The Ottawa nursery organizers decided, in 1916, that the number of children attending would be limited to forty, "as [there was] no room for more, and not enough staff."[36]

The number of children attending the nurseries varied according to the availability of employment for women and the prevalence of disease in the city. When employment for women was high and rates of disease low, the nurseries had a greater number of children attending than when women's employment possibilities were low or disease prevalent. Table 2.3 sets out the average, greatest and least number of children attending the East End Day Nursery for selected months. These are representative of attendance for the years 1903 to 1909 and 1924 to 1926. Attendance ranged from six or eight children to 100 or 130, with averages of forty to sixty children daily. The difference between the greatest and least was very wide, and the average does not represent the true numbers of children. For example, in February 1909 the average daily attendance was sixty-two children but there were 106 children on at least one day, and only twenty on another.

The regularity of individual children's attendance also varied according to mothers' employment and children's illness,

Table 2.3. Average, Greatest and Least Number of Children Attending the East End Day Nursery for Selected Months

Date	Average Daily	Greatest Daily	Least Daily
July 1903	23	32	9
Sept 1904	47	65	16
Feb 1905	24	45	6
Jan 1906	36	53	14
Nov 1906	72	106	27
March 1907	52	77	16
May 1908	103	149	30
Feb 1909	62	106	20
Oct 1924	102	129	32
Jan 1925	57	81	14
Oct 1925	99	129	33
March 1926	72	92	23

Source: EEDN. Minutes 1903 to 1909; 1924 to 1926.

making it impossible to predict who would arrive for care. The organizers of the Montreal Day Nursery perceived these large and fluctuating numbers of children as a problem of managing the nursery day, not of providing good caregiving:

> The regularity, possible in the management of other Institutions was lacking, for every morning there was an uncertainty as to the size of the family, and the ages to be cared for.
>
> Occasionally there were as few as forty, at other times there were ninety-five, when forty-five of that number were under four [years]. Just to keep such a family amply fed, needed constant planning, not to think of the patient preserving work required to administer to all the other necessities.[37]

Similar to the fluctuations in daily attendance, children often did not continue in the nursery from month to month. For example, at the East End Day Nursery in 1935, twenty-nine children attended in January; in February, fourteen of these did not return and one new child attended; in May, thirty-one children attended but only nine had continued from February, six who had attended in January but not in February, returned, and there were sixteen new children.[38]

Each of the day nurseries was originally established within single rooms of houses, in which the children's activities of playing, eating, and sleeping occurred without separation. Areas were differentiated by their materials and equipment, but concurrent use of space and multiple use of materials was carried out, such as at the East End nursery during its first few years, when the infants and nurses were in "one room where they lived all day and even the cooking was done in the same room."[39]

In the early 1900s the nurseries were moved into large houses. With the greater space provided by the houses, the nurseries were able to separate activities such as eating and playing, and children according to age by having different play areas for school age children and for younger children. It is important to realize that activities and age groups were not separated to enhance child development. Rather, such divisions were carried out to ensure the safety of the younger children by protecting them from the more active, older children.

Even in the large houses, preschool children and infants occupied the same rooms, and the cots and cribs of these younger children were located in the same rooms in which they played. A newspaper article on the Montreal Day Nursery described the young children's room as containing cots and high chairs occupied by infants, alongside the two, three and four year olds playing with bricks and dolls.[40] An article about the Winnipeg nursery in the 1930s provided a similar account of nursery organization:

> A well-aired sunny room, clean and well kept, where the children play, there are high chairs, a long table with small chairs, and a few toys, conspicuous amongst them a gray teddy bear.... A baby carriage in one corner furnishes a haven of rest for a sleepy baby....
> The larger children sat expectantly at the table. It was approaching half-past eleven. Soon the assistant came in with white enamel soup plates with blue edges.... These are the self-feeders.[41]

At all the nurseries, outdoor play space consisted of a yard adjacent to the houses with such equipment as sandboxes, slides,

East End Day Nursery (no date). Child with play phone.

and see-saws. This area was used by the older children while the youngest ones, for safety reasons, played on a screened verandah.

Toys were scarce, and they do not appear to have been a major concern of the nursery organizers. Their provision relied largely on donations by companies and individuals of items such as picture books, toys, and blocks. In 1920 the Montreal nursery accepted the donation of a table gramophone and six records, as well as a $30 cheque for the buying of records and books. That the organizers of this nursery regarded play as a natural feature of childhood but not a necessary part of day nursery care is revealed by the comment regarding the donations. An organizer remarked, "These are a few of the amusements, for the children must play, but it ought not to be over-looked that at all times, it is the constant endeavour of the Committee and Staff to afford instruction in matters of conduct, such as cleanliness, obedience and good manners."[42]

The preceding description of early day nursery care provides a sketch of the relationship between the agencies' role in providing social services for mothers, and the beliefs about day nursery caregiving. What is apparent is the lack of detail on the policies and practices of their activities. This is not so much a matter of incomplete records, but of what was considered important to record, and therefore, what was considered essential in the care of children.

In their role as social service agencies, the day nurseries provided child care to destitute families so the mother could obtain employment. Beliefs and values during this period emphasized children's competency and independence. The role of caregivers was to ensure an environment that provided for children's physical health and safety and for their moral guidance. However, the beliefs and values about children that governed the role of these nurseries would be dramatically changed as the twentieth century wore on.

FOOTNOTES

1 MDN. "Annual Report of the Day Nursery and Industrial School Montreal, 1890." Emphasis in original. Citations to MDN, refer to archival material on the Montreal Day Nursery. Pat Schulz Collection located at the Baldwin Room, Metropolitan Toronto Reference Library, Canada.

2 For a class analysis of the Toronto and Montreal nursery organizers see Schulz, 1978.

3 MDN. Typed manuscript, c. 1927.

4 Settlement houses were similar in many respects to present day community centres, but with a much more extensive mandate and provision of services. Located in the poorer areas of cities, settlement houses were intended to provide educational, social and recreational services to neighbourhood residents. These included such activities as sports clubs for all ages, sewing

clubs for women, and adult education programs. They were viewed by their organizers as centres for enriching residents in the basics of democracy and citizenship.

5 VDN. "History of the Victoria Day Nursery." Citations to VDN refer to archival material on the Victoria Day Nursery. Pat Schulz Collection located at the Baldwin Room, Metropolitan Toronto Reference Library, Canada.

6 VDN. "History Victoria Day Care."

7 WDN. Program of Meeting, 1912-1913. Citations to WDN refer to archival material for the Winnipeg nursery. Mothers' Association Collection, located at the Provincial Archives of Manitoba, Winnipeg, Canada.

8 ODN. Handwritten History, no date by Mrs. Cassels. Citations to ODN refer to archival material on the Ottawa Day Nursery. Andrew Fleck Child Centre Collection, located at the National Archives of Canada, Manuscript Division, Ottawa, Canada.

9 ODN. "Praise Mrs. A.W. Fleck for Day Nursery Work" newspaper article c. 1938.

10 MDN. Annual Report, 1898.

11 MDN. Minutes, 1906.

12 Personal Communication.

13 Initiated primarily in the late 1800s, well-baby clinics were set up in poorer neighbourhoods to provide free basic medical services to pregnant women, infants and young children. This included the provision of health checks, pure milk or formulas, and parenting classes.

14 ODN. Annual Report, 1920-21.

15 EEDN. Annual Meeting, 1952. Citations to EEDN refer to archival material for the East End Day Nursery. East End Day Nursery Collection, located at the Baldwin Room, Metropolitan Toronto Reference Library, Canada.

16 EEDN. Minutes, December 4, 1911.

17 MDN. Annual Report, 1912.

18 WDN. Minutes, February 19, 1913.

19 EEDN. Minutes, December 4, 1916.

20 All references to Maizie Hill are based on an interview carried out by the author in 1993. Maizie Hill attended the Ottawa Day Nursery as an infant and child from the time her mother was that nursery's cook in 1929. Ms. Hill also worked at the nursery for a summer in the mid-1940s.

21 ODN. "Mothers Having War Jobs Find Day Nursery a Haven" newspaper article, July 24, 1942.

22 MDN. Annual Report, 1906.

23 MDN. Annual Report, 1907.

24 MDN. Annual Report, 1890.

25 "Taking Care of Babies" *Family Herald and Weekly Star* [Montreal], April 20, 1904.

26 Hill, 1993. Interview.

27 WEC. "History of West End Creche," 1974. Citations to WEC, refer to archival material on the West End Creche. Pat Schulz Collection, located at the Baldwin Room, Metropolitan Toronto Reference Library, Canada.

28 ODN. Annual Report, 1917.

29 "Day Nursery Children Need Your Help" *Winnipeg Free Press*, October 14, 1939.

30 "Taking Care of Babies" 1904.

31 "Service of Day Nursery Unique" *The Citizen* [Ottawa], February 11, 1925. The number of children attending per year was calculated by counting the number of individual children who attended the nursery for every day that the nursery provided service. For example, twenty children attending for twenty days a month for twelve months would be calculated as 20 X 20 X 12 = 4800 children.

32 MDN. Annual Report, 1912.

33 EEDN. Minutes, 1892.

34 "Something Novel for Dollar Days" *The Citizen* [Ottawa], February 10, 1925.

35 "Day Nursery Children Need Your Help" *Winnipeg Free Press*, October 14, 1939.

36 ODN. Minutes, April 4, 1916.

37 MDN. Minutes of the Annual Meeting, 1919.

38 EEDN. Attendance Records, 1935.

39 EEDN. Annual Report, 1952.

40 "Taking care of babies" 1904.

41 WDN. "The Day Nursery: A Winnipeg Institution that Helps People to Help Themselves." newspaper article, c. 1930s.

42 MDN. Annual Report, 1920.

Chapter Three

Constructing the New Child

Today the pre-school child is assuming an unique importance for science. The problems of development as focused in the young normal child are of interest not merely for parents and educators but also for those whose business it is to study the laws of health, nutrition, physical and mental growth, habit formation and the influence of the group upon the behaviour of the individual. In the average home these problems exist, but not the opportunity for their study and solution.[1]

The early years of the twentieth century was a period that conceived and brought together new ways of thinking about children, with new ways of studying them, and with new ways of caring for and schooling them. Based on theories of genetic and psychological development, the new ideas about children would effectively transform ideas about the nature of childhood.

Scientific Child Study

The quote at the beginning of this chapter highlights the ideas about childhood that became prominent from the 1920s. It was believed that *scientific* investigation of development would provide essential knowledge about children, enabling the solving of 'problems of development' — that is, knowing what are the typical behaviours displayed at particular ages, and what promoted or inhibited them. The recommended sites for such study were to be the specialized environments of university nursery schools. It was proposed that the outcome of scientific child study in nursery school settings would reveal genetic patterns of child development and show how children's environments could be arranged in order to ensure that optimal development occurred.

The belief in the role of scientific child study for answering questions about development and its management was an extension of the late nineteenth century research of G. Stanley Hall.[2] Hall was the first scholar to approach childhood as a serious object of academic (rather than personal) study. While his topic of interest was childhood, he gathered data primarily from adults through the use of questionnaires. It was mostly teachers who responded to the surveys by providing memories of their own childhoods, and their observations of children in their classrooms. Between 1894 and 1915, he conducted 194 surveys on different topics of study. An idea of the vast quantity of his research is arrived at from knowing that for just the years 1894 to 1896, he conducted thirty-one different surveys, with *each* survey being sent to approximately 800 respondents, providing a total distribution of about 27,200 questionnaires.[3] The anecdotal reports obtained from his surveys resulted in revelations about children and childhood, demonstrating that children were not just 'less' than adults in their physical and mental abilities, but that they thought in a manner different from adults.

Hall has been credited with establishing the study of children as a legitimate focus within psychology and for gaining the widespread interest and participation of parents and teachers in the study of childhood. However, the qualitative nature of his method and the large amount of data collected limited interpretations to general descriptive statements of children's interests and abilities at certain ages. He was unable to achieve his goal of discovering a genetic schedule of development. Furthermore, Hall's method of study was criticized as unscientific because he did not use objective and systematic observation and recording procedures of children themselves, and because his data could not be quantified.

It was Hall's former student, Arnold Gesell, who provided the impetus and framework for the next, scientific, phase of child study. Gesell undertook extensive observations of children using systematic procedures. His work came to the forefront of child study in 1925, when he published the first 'norms' of development for children from birth to age five.[4] Gesell organized his data about children's behaviours into schedules of growth in the areas of motor, language, adaptive (behaviours considered to be demonstrated prior to the development of 'intelligence'), and personal-social development. In constructing the developmental schedules, Gesell achieved what Hall could not, a timetable of normative chronological changes in children's emotional, social, physical and mental abilities.

Gesell's schedules of development provided more than a record of the natural path of human growth, they transformed ways of thinking about the period of life called childhood. His division of children's development into progressive stages characterized childhood as a passage through a series of distinctive but accumulative features. According to this conception, normal child development consists of movement from one stage to another within a specified period of time. A current stage of development is the manifestation of the successful completion and retention of past stages. Normal development requires that a stage be completed before the next, the future, stage can be acquired.

For Gesell and other maturationists, the purpose of the schedules was not just their usefulness for observing the current and changing status of an individual child or group of children, but in providing a frame of reference for investigating details of human growth and behaviours that were then used to construct methods of care which were supposed to optimize development. Gesell identified this application as *developmental supervision*, and defined it as follows:

> A consecutive series of developmental diagnoses and inventories in which a cumulative knowledge of the child is made the basis of safeguarding his development.... Developmental supervision embraces the total physical and mental development of the child.[5]

Gesell's contribution to child study was immensely significant. Having obtained his data through standardized observations and systematic recording procedures, his research was hailed as meeting the criteria of real science, and defined the procedures for studying children that were modeled through-

Figure 3.1. Examples from Gesell's Abridged Developmental Schedules

Motor Characteristics

Four Months	Prefers to lie on back. Tries to raise self; lifting head and shoulders. Can roll from side to back (or back to side). Holds head erect when carried.
Four Years	Draws cross from copy. Traces diamond path. Hooks fish in 15 or 30 seconds with right or left hand.

Language

Four Months	Coos. Smiles. Laughs aloud. Makes several vocalizations.
Four Years	Distinguishes four prepositions. Uses descriptive word with picture. Repeats twelve syllables.

Adaptive Behaviour

Four Months	Notices large objects. May notice spoon on table. Hands react to table.
Four Years	Folds paper diagonally. Draws three completions in incomplete man. Completes patience picture. Puts two blocks in cup.

Personal-Social Behaviour

Four Months	Shows selective interest in animated face. Makes anticipatory postural adjustment on being lifted. Turns head to voice. Plays with hands.
Four Years	Uses building material constructively. Buttons clothes. Goes on errands outside of house. Washes self.

Source: Gesell, A. 1925/1928. *The Mental Growth of the Pre-School Child.* NY: MacMillan, pp. 278; 383-384.

out North America. The relationship he defined as occurring between children's chronological age and their abilities provided the basis for comparative studies of children and the framework for future child study research. This way of thinking about children is accepted as 'commonsense' in late twentieth century Western societies. Everyday applications of developmental schedules are found in the labelling of children's toys in terms of age appropriateness, and the constant references to developmental norms in parenting television programs, books and magazines. The extent to which developmental schedules have become a part of childhood discourse makes it difficult to realize that prior to the 1920s, childhood was not discussed in these terms. It was not that people did not *know* that children changed as they grew older, but that never before had children's behaviour for specific age periods been numerically standardized, and presented as the model of childhood itself.

Beyond Gesell's creation of scientific child study research and the maturation theory of development, his findings were applied, by him as well as others, to systems of care for young children.

The Mental Hygiene Orientation

During the same period of time that scientific child study was creating new ideas about development, the mental hygiene movement began to focus on the early years of childhood. The term 'mental hygiene' refers to a concern about personality formation. The mental hygiene movement was organized at the beginning of the twentieth century with the belief that most individuals lived lives that were not conducive to optimum personality development, and that the resulting lack of mental health of individuals was a threat to the well-being of civilization. The concept of adjustment was central to the mental hygiene orientation from the 1920s in Canada.[6] It referred to the ability of individuals to adapt their personalities (ways of thinking, feeling, and acting) to the multiple requirements of society. Persons needed to adapt to the different social structures and institutions in which they lived at various stages of their lives. There were the demands of adjustment to be made to the school as student or teacher, to the family as child or as parent, to the workplace as employee or employer. 'Optimal adjustment' was the sign of a 'wholesome' personality, and it required that the individual demonstrate no extremes in behaviour; for example, to be neither too introverted nor too extroverted, to be neither too fearful nor dangerously fearless. Maladjusted and unadjusted personalities were individuals who demonstrated incorrect social behaviours, such as teenage girls' participation in delinquent behaviours.[7] In the maladjusted state the individual had learned incorrect 'habits' of behaviour; in the unadjusted state the individual had not had the opportunity to learn the correct habits of living. For both 'conditions,' the individuals affected needed to adjust their personalities to a normal status; the unadjusted, by learning the behaviours necessary for satisfactory social relations; the maladjusted, by replacing bad habits with good ones.

The theories of two major twentieth century psychoanalysts were at the forefront of the application of mental hygiene principles to children. Sigmund Freud's identification of childhood as the period of development when the individual's personality was formed — for life, and Adolf Meyer's argument that personality could be reformed during the early years of development, made childhood the "critical point of attack" against mental illness.[8] When these two theories were brought together within the mental hygiene orientation, the early years of life were seen as the period when prevention of later psychosis was both possible and necessary. The assumption was that the earlier the child could be brought up according to mental hygiene principles, the more positive the outlook for successful adult adjustment.

Child Development and Mental Hygiene through Nursery School Care

Arnold Gesell played a key role in the initial linking of scientific child study to mental hygiene principles in his arguments for preschool child care. He warned that the rapidity of the development of the young child's mind, character formation, and "habits of living" during the pre-school years required parents to "catch" the infant's character in order to form it appropriately.[9] He described the development as follows:

The infant learns to see, to hear, handle, walk, comprehend, and talk. He acquires an uncountable number of habits fundamental to the complex act of living. Never again will his mind, his character, his spirit advance as rapidly as in this formative pre-school period of growth. Never again will we have an equal chance to lay the foundations of mental health. From the standpoint of mental hygiene the pre-school period, therefore, appears to have no less significance than it has for physical vigor and survival.[10]

Gesell's incorporation of his developmental studies within the mental hygiene orientation created a frame for the next thirty years of child study work, and provided the basis of a new approach to child care.

The connection between the nursery school, scientific child study, and 'expert' care was proposed as crucial to the formation of a healthy society. Nursery school therefore had to be available to all children. The preschool age was perceived to have been by-passed in the state's provision of services for children. The nursery school was to remedy this situation by extending downward in age the "developmental safeguards" that were available to children attending grade school.[11] It was through the provision of nursery school child care that the scientific study of the child and the management of children's development by the application of mentally hygienic care would be combined for the preschool years. North American nursery schools were initially organized to provide both the controlled environment deemed necessary for identifying normal development and for its optimization.

University of Toronto Institute of Child Study

In North America, the connection between the multiple ideas of mental hygiene, child study, nursery school and child care was made through the founding of model child study institutions (those with a nursery school, university affiliation and a mental hygiene orientation) with the financial support of the Laura Spelman Rockefeller Memorial Foundation. One of these was the University of Toronto Institute of Child Study (initially known as the St. George's School for Child Study) founded in 1925. The Toronto Institute was originally a division of the

Department of Psychology at the University of Toronto. William Emet Blatz, a Master's graduate of the University of Toronto and new graduate of doctoral studies in psychology at the University of Chicago, was appointed as its first Director. He held that position until his retirement in 1960. In 1938, the Institute became an autonomous department within the University of Toronto.[12]

The Institute was organized into the St. George's Nursery School, and the Parent Education Division. Within each of these departments, Institute faculty undertook graduate training and applied research. The nursery school was designed as a laboratory for observing children's behaviour and development, for carrying out experimental methods of child care, and for providing a model of care for parents and other caregivers. The Institute's nursery school setting was considered ideal for research because the environment could be controlled and manipulated. As with other child study research from the 1920s to the 1970s, the emphasis was on observing children in situations designed to promote certain types of development and behaviours. As a research institute concerned with normal child development within the specialized environment of the nursery school, admission was limited to children who could 'satisfactorily adjust' to the demands of routines and independent activity; in other words, the typically developing and mentally healthy child. The Parent Education Division was created both for learning from parents about the behaviours of children in their home environment and for providing parents with up-to-date information on child development and methods of child care. Parents of children enrolled in the Institute's nursery school were required to attend parent education meetings conducted by Institute faculty or graduate students, and to keep records of their children's development and behaviours. The Institute's nursery school was the hub of the program, for through it both purposes of child study research and parent education were to be achieved. Because of the centrality of its nursery school in the activities of the Institute, and because it acted as a model for later nursery schools and day nurseries, this chapter will focus on that aspect of the Institute's work.

The families who enrolled their children in the Institute's nursery school have been identified as unique in their interest in child development and willingness to learn new methods of child training.[13] From Institute records maintained for the years 1925-26, 1926-27, 1928 and 1960, the families' socio-economic characteristics can be identified.[14] For those years, the children's fathers were doctors, professors, and "other professionals;" their mothers had high school or advanced education, and before marriage had worked as teachers or as secretaries. The average age range of the mothers was from thirty-two to thirty-five years and thirty-seven to forty-five years; the average age range for the fathers was from forty-one to forty-four years. The majority of the parents were Canadian born and the families had only one or two children.

The families who enrolled their children in the Institute's nursery school were, until the 1940s, going against the norm of middle class caregiving. It was expected that mothers of this socio-economic group would care for their own children, and not doing so was criticized as an abandonment of the family. The Institute made continuous efforts to assure the public that it was not relieving mothers of their duty, but was providing training so they could better carry out their roles. Group care of middle class children was also unusual because of the prevalence, until the 1950s, of deadly and debilitating disease in children's group care. The Institute's nursery school implemented a number of measures to reduce the risk of contagious diseases: group size was kept very small; all children were examined by a nurse before they entered the playroom; any child showing symptoms of fever or illness was not allowed to attend. The oddity of the Institute's nursery school as an institution for young children and the health risk of group care were the primary reasons for a low enrolment of six children at its opening. By the 1930s its success at maintaining children's health and its publicized aim of training mothers in child care contributed to broad enough acceptance to assure a full enrolment of thirty some children and a waiting list of prospective children.

The Child Care Curriculum of the Institute's Nursery School

It was through the Institute's nursery school that the ideas of maturation theory and mental hygiene were applied in what I have termed a normative child care curriculum. Based on the

47

mental hygiene orientation, the curriculum was structured to enhance optimum psychological adjustment in the early years of childhood. In addition, based on the maturation theory of child development, the curriculum was designed to manage and direct children's behaviours so as to ensure efficient genetic development. The concept of childhood formulated within this curriculum was that the first six years of life were the first of many periods of development leading to adulthood. This was a time of preparation, during which the individual was to learn how to make positive social and mental adjustments, to acquire 'habits' of personal care in order to satisfy bodily needs, and to gain knowledge about, and experiences in, the world while "learning to adjust himself to a rapidly enlarging social environment."[15] The organization of time, space, observation and adult-child interactions were four features of the Institute's nursery school normative curriculum that were the leading elements in the provision of child care. The curriculum set out in detail when children should be carrying out particular behaviours (temporal structures), where those behaviours should be carried out (spatial structures), how development should be supervised (observational structures), and how adults should respond to children (interactional structures).[16]

Normative Temporal Structures

In conceptualizing the maturation of children as a series of progressive stages development was organized as linear time. Earlier in this chapter, it was explained how, with the creation of developmental schedules, normal child development was understood as moving progressively from one stage to the next. While this temporal pattern was viewed as genetic in origin, and therefore a natural process, it was also argued that adequate environmental factors had to be present in order for nature to take its course. In the child care curriculum of the Institute's nursery school, time was organized for the purpose of managing this genetic path of linear development.

One of the methods used to manage temporal development was the division of children into age specific groups. When the day nurseries were in spacious locations, the children attending were divided into two broad age groups: school age and preschool age (including infants). This division was based on safety concerns, keeping the larger and more active older ones apart from the younger ones. At the Institute's nursery school the age division of children was narrower and had a different rationale. Children were grouped by the age categories of two to three-and-a-half, and three and a half to five years, or two, three, four, and five years, depending upon the availability of children to make up the groups. These age groups were provided with temporal labels that designated their placement along the linear and hierarchical range of development; the youngest groups of children were the 'juniors' and the oldest groups were the 'seniors.'

While the division of children into these age categories was unique for the organization of the day nurseries, more important were the maturationist and mental hygiene explanations for the categorization. Child study research had determined that children of the same chronological age demonstrated similar abilities and thus, they were designated as having similar needs. From the mental hygiene perspective, children were also identified as requiring the experience of living with others of the same age, because like-age groups provided opportunities for "naturally" learning how to get along with contemporaries.[17] It was from these explanations that the practice and ideology of the temporal management of children through age categories could be exported to the day nurseries.

Time at the nursery school was structured into routines for the purpose of managing children's linear temporal development. To fully appreciate this way of thinking, it is necessary to understand the early twentieth century concept of 'habit.' It . was argued that habits were formed from the child's participation within a structured environment. From the maturationist perspective, habits were viewed as the internalization (habituation) of the child's external responses to demands of the environment, including the demands made by adults such as how to eat, how to wash, how to eliminate. Habits were considered essential for relieving the individual from having to constantly think about how regular daily activities were carried out, thereby reducing the 'waste' of developmental energy sources.

From the mental hygiene orientation, the formation of correct habits occurred through experiencing regulated daily routines. Habits learned through routines would provide for mental health by reducing emotional tension between adults and children that occurred during conflicts over the when and how of everyday activities. In their book for parents on child rearing, Blatz and his co-author Helen Bott outlined this perspective:

> The child who rises, dresses and eats his meals promptly, who sleeps at the right time and who is well-regulated in his eliminative functions, suffers from a minimum of restraint by reason of these necessary duties — the rest of his time is set free for play. Also emotional conflict and its attendant frustration is largely eliminated when the child has learned to cooperate readily in the prescribed routine.[18]

It was through the temporal curriculum of routines at the Institute's nursery school, that the management of children's development through habit formation was applied. During routine activities the child was expected to carry out tasks of personal care and bodily satisfaction such as eating, sleeping, and eliminating. Through the routinization of activities, children had the opportunity to succeed in their individual linear development by trying activities over and over again. In this way, children would internalize the social rules governing activities, and thereby avoid both waste of developmental energy and the formation of maladjusted personalities.

The timetable of the nursery school was the Institute's tool for ensuring that development was managed by routinization. The specific and consistent ordering of time was presented as a method by which the nursery school teacher could ensure children's efficient development. Within the nursery school day of 8:45 a.m. to 3:00 p.m., were multiple intervals of five, ten, fifteen, thirty, thirty-five, forty-five minutes, and two hours. The density of the Institute's nursery school timetable indicates the extent to which it was meant to structure the child's day, and thereby the child's development. The structure of the timetable and the activities that were to occur within each unit of time was as follows (the overlapping of time indicates the movement of small groups of children into various activities, that is, all children were not moved into different activities at the same time):[19]

8:45 - 9:30	Nurse's Inspection and Entrance Routine
9:00 - 9:30	Elimination Routine (drink of water and attempt to urinate)
9:00 - 11:00	Outdoor Free Play Period
10:30 - 11:00	Putting Away Toys
10:30 - 11:00	Cloakroom Routine (undressing)
10:30 - 11:00	Elimination Routine (attempt to urinate)
10:30 - 11:00	Mid-morning Nourishment (1/2 glass of tomato juice)
11:00 - 11:35	Indoor Free Play Period
11:00 - 11:35	Washing Routine
11:00 - 11:35	Carpentry
11:30 - 11:35	Putting Away Toys
11:35 - 11:50	Organized Group Play (story-telling, music, conversation)
11:50 - 12:00	Relaxation Routine
12:00 - 12:30	Dining Room Routine
12:30 - 12:45	Elimination Routine
12:30 - 2:30	Sleeping Routine
2:30 - 2:45	Elimination Routine
2:30 - 3:00	Dressing Routine
2:45 - 3:00	Mid-afternoon Nourishment (glass of milk)
2:45 - 3:00	Parents Call for Children

The importance of maintaining the schedule was emphasized, and this became the responsibility of the nursery school teacher:

> Arrangements should be made within the present staff to keep this timetable workable at all times. When emergency arises, provision should be made to have gaps filled, regardless of all other work.[20]

A departure from the schedule was allowed for individual children when deemed necessary, such as for gradually 'adjusting' children to its requirements. However, the division of activities into specific temporal units was presented as an essential component in the overall developmental management of children.

For instance, a scheduled washroom time was intended to prevent, as much as possible, an interruption of children's play.

Each routine activity had a set developmental problem that the child had to solve, such as washing one's face, taking off one's coat, or lying quietly in bed. The problem was set by the adult according to each child's ability to solve it, allowing sufficient time for the child to attempt it and ensuring a minimum of confusion, excitement or distraction. Every moment within each of the intervals of time, had a defined purpose whereby a number of actions or procedures were to be carried out by the child. For example, directions for the washing routine were as follows:

> Each child is directed individually to the washroom. Not more than four wash at any one time (two junior and two senior children). A definite washing procedure is followed. (Washing hands, changing water, washing face, drying hands and face, combing hair).[21]

"Unacceptable behaviours" by children during routines, such as playing, dawdling and inattention, were perceived as preventing the necessary development of a "businesslike attitude toward routine requirements."[22] In response, temporal behaviour management techniques were employed. The child was to be removed from the group, given personal assistance in completing the routine activity, and advised that he or she was apparently not able to carry out the routine. In some cases it was advised that a senior child be temporarily moved to the junior group. These actions were intended to inform the child that he or she had failed to independently achieve sufficient development; removal to the younger age group was an explicit temporal 'demotion' of the child to a younger developmental level.

In comparison to the use of time in the day nurseries during the early years of the twentieth century, the Institute's specification of detailed ways of carrying out day-to-day activities reconstituted them as specialized skills that needed to be taught to the children by trained nursery school teachers. The detailed instructions for carrying out the routines left no room for ambiguity in action, and therefore the possibility of ambiguous development. With this itemized organization of children's movements the

Institute's nursery school would achieve Gesell's concept of catching development in order to manage it according to the norms set out in the developmental schedules.

Normative Spatial Structures

Along with temporal structures, the child care curriculum of the Institute's nursery school was organized in terms of normative spatial structures. The nursery school was distinct from other places for children, including the family home, through its arrangement, use and meaning of materials and space. The internal and external spatial designations of the nursery school

University of Toronto Institute of Child Study, Nursery School, c. 1930s.
Play Room: Areas of the play room were designated for certain types of activities.
The fence around the house centre was a physical boundary to help
children keep their play activities separate.

University of Toronto Institute of Child Study, Nursery School, c. 1930s.
Outdoor Playground: Play equipment was spread out so children would
distinguish between different types of play.
Equipment was selected to match the age abilities of the children.

were conceived not only to allow for specialized caregiving, but just as with temporal organization, everything having to do with spatial arrangements was rationalized in terms of maturation theory and mental hygiene.

Unlike the use of space during the early years of the day nurseries, areas of the Institute's nursery school were organized for particular kinds of activities and in this way, space was intended to manage children's development. Outdoors, materials such as swings, sand boxes and climbers, were arranged so as to scatter children's play over the available space. Indoors, space was arranged according to strenuous or quiet occupations as well as by types of play materials. For example, dolls were to have their own area, trucks and cars another. By the availability of the materials and equipment, such as toys for play and items for personal care, children were to be made aware of the kinds of activities that were to take place within the spaces. It was argued that this would promote mentally hygienic habits of play behaviour by making "attention and concentration easier for the child by lessening the distracting influence of other children and other toys, as well as diminishing general confusion and social upsets by dividing the children into groups each with a particular interest."[23] Cooperative play, project work, and suggestions for new uses of material would be produced through arranging related materials and toys near one another. While the enhancement of play opportunities through the combining of various materials was recognized, greater importance was placed on the separation of "units of occupation," as Blatz and his colleagues called them, for developmental purposes. For example,

> 'Playing house' and 'pasting' do not mix. Nor do plasticine and dolls. So the layout of the child's play space should be such that these distinctions are appreciated and he learns to choose each occupation and to play it to the full before proceeding to another. A jumble of toys leads naturally to a jumbled and distracted method of play.[24]

The problem with such play was its assumed link to a jumbled and distracted method of living. Through orderliness the child's behaviours would not be directionless, but would correspond, through each moment of play, with the larger movement forward in development.

Whereas in the day nurseries, children were cared for in different areas for convenience and safety, within the Institute's nursery school space was organized to incorporate developmental time by the provision of areas for different ages, "wholly adjusted to the child's size and scale of capacities."[25] All the materials were to be of child size so that children could independently make choices, get what they needed, and put items away when finished. Freedom of access to materials was associated with providing children with opportunities for the promotion of positive mental hygiene qualities such as independence, self-expression and achievement.

It was in the relationship between the age of the child and the materials available at the Institute's nursery school that the teachers attempted to manage the complete development of the children at each age level, and to promote movement from one stage to the next. Play materials were classified according to their appropriateness for use by children in each age group, and children's play with the materials was managed according to their chronological ages. Two-year-olds were to have play things that both met and encouraged the development of two year old capabilities; five-year-olds required materials that demanded more complex skills and behaviours.[26]

The nursery school teachers were to supervise the children's use of the materials and space to ensure the expression of developmentally appropriate behaviours. Materials were not to be set

University of Toronto Institute of Child Study, Nursery School, c. 1930s.
Dining Area: Children sat in small groups at child size tables with a nursery school teacher,
who supervised and managed their development of eating habits.

up in the space and then left for chance opportunities for children's activities. The adult was responsible for ensuring the materials available met the developmental needs of each child, and that they were used according to the child's capacities. Always the nursery school teacher was responsible for planning space so as to ensure children's forward developmental movement:

> If the adult has not some general plan in mind with regard to her equipment, there is danger that the child will attempt something beyond his ability, and find himself at a complete loss or, on the other hand, fail to see how he can proceed to more advanced play after the first steps have been mastered.[27]

The use of space during the early years of the day nurseries was based on issues such as availability and usability. In contrast, the curriculum of the Institute's nursery school conceptualized space in an entirely new way. It was transformed into a feature of the environment that would itself manage development.

Normative Observation

Within the Institute's nursery school, time and space were organized to manage genetic and mental hygiene development, but management was just part of the equation. It was through the supervision of development that it would be made known whether or not the child was 'on schedule.' The method and use of normative observation was a unique feature in the care of children. In early day nursery care observation and record keeping was kept to a minimum because it was not thought to be an integral element of child care. This changed with the Institute's curriculum. From the 1920s, training in methods of observation and record keeping was considered necessary for the appropriate care of the child:

> Unless there is very careful guidance in evaluating children's activities together with their habits, attitudes, and achievements, freedom may degenerate into license, and child expression and initiative lead to trivial and unorganized activities which fail to arrive at results which are developing to the individual, which challenge him to put forth his best efforts, and which have definite social values.[28]

Institute nursery school teachers were to engage in continuous observation and record keeping of children's behaviours in order to supervise their development. Information obtained from the observation records were used to assess and plan for individual children's developmental progress. Collectively, they were used to compare the behaviour of different children and to establish norms for various aspects of childhood development.

In order to supervise the developmentally appropriate use of materials, space was organized to ensure that there were no areas where children could be out of sight of the teachers. Children were never to be on their own, there could be no dividers in the rooms that could not be seen over, and even the washroom stalls were to be open. The teachers were expected to "be alert to every move of the group, and of individual children."[29] Mary J. Wright, a graduate of the Institute, and prominent child study researcher, summarized the Institute's influence over spatial arrangements: "It was Blatz who first took the doors off the toilet cubicles in the nursery school ... and it is he who *is* responsible for the prominent places which toilets occupy in the Ontario child care centres of today."[30] In addition to the design of the children's areas, special rooms were built within the nursery so that observers such as parents, visitors and research scientists, could watch the children without being seen by them.

Daily records on all children were kept for attendance, nurse's examination, sleeping, eating and elimination. The latter three were to be conveyed to the parents when they arrived at the end of the day. Intermittent records allowed for the systematic evaluation of development and specialized records would be gathered if there was the suggestion of a problem in behaviour or development, such as "if the child's motor development appears to be

University of Toronto Institute of Child Study, Nursery School, c. 1930s.
Observation of children during their washing routine.
Child-size sinks were to encourage independence.

University of Toronto Institute of Child Study, Nursery School, c. 1930s.
Women are watching the children through an observation screen.

poor, an examination of his washing and dining room records will indicate his skill in handling and carrying objects, as exercised in these periods."[31] Observations during play time documented children's use of the materials and "general habits of concentration and interest and in constructive ability."[32] Information about social behaviour was gathered for the purpose of indicating the child's adjustment to the group. As well, records were kept of children's emotional and disciplinary behaviours. At the end of the month a measure of each individual's developmental progress was calculated from the summary scoring of the observations.

It was through the application of systematic observation and record keeping that children's development could be measured and assessed against standards of normative progress. Such recording of observations was thought to provide an "objective and factual" picture of each child's complete development, that could early on identify when and how the child deviated from the norm, failed to develop or "lapsed" in "efficient" development.[33] The records were presented as a scientific method of child care by guarding against casual observations leading to the imagining of problems or the making of invalid conclusions.[34]

Dorothy Millichamp has commented on the relevance of the records in the early years of the school in the construction of new beliefs about child development. Note that 'knowledge' of children's development outside the context of scientific research was dismissed. This was the subordination of personal knowledge of children to scientifically created, and therefore 'relevant,' knowledge.

> Everything in the 1930s was a discovery. No one knew a single thing about children's sleeping habits, etc., except by a single parent of a single child.... No one knew what was happening in nursery schools. All those records we kept on routines, which people now laugh at, were to discover not what one child does, but thirty to fifty.... They were the first discovery of routine patterns.[35]

Normative observation also had implications for the subjective formation of the child's caregiver. The nursery school teachers generally carried out their observational record keeping within sight of the children. The very process of keeping observation records while caring for the children forced the nursery school teachers to be physically separate from the children and thus to implement the desired curriculum of independent learning.

The Institute's nursery school teacher's use of these methods enabled her to see herself as more than a 'minder' of the child. She perceived herself as a scientific supervisor of development. It also made her consider herself key to the child's development. If the child's development progressed, she was a successful teacher. If the child did not move forward in developmental time or regressed, she needed to determine the reasons. Perhaps her method was in error, or perhaps the child's parent's were inadequate caregivers. Her task was then to intervene in the spatial or temporal environment or change her own behaviour.

Normative Interaction
In addition to the use of explicit rules about time and space

organization, interactions between the child and nursery school teacher were viewed as influencing children's knowledge about the means and ends of social behaviour. The teacher's physical movements, voice, and 'manner' were calculated to keep children's attention on their own actions, rather than on those of the adult. The nursery school teacher's behaviours were to follow established procedures so as to provide consistency in care from one person to the next. The guidelines for the teachers were as follows:

> The adults should be as inconspicuous as possible, moving only when necessary and then without hurry. Sitting down whenever possible on a low chair is a good rule to establish. The children should always be spoken to slowly and quietly and in a matter-of-fact tones. It is advisable on the whole not to initiate conversation during the routines as this is too distracting for the child. One is, of course, always pleasant and interested.[36]

Teachers were to be impersonal when directing children through routines, so that the children would take on responsibility for the completion of tasks. They would point out a child's mistakes to her or him, and direct the child towards easier and better procedures, using physical rather than verbal directions, and giving suggestions rather than commands. In disciplining a child for unacceptable behaviour, the teacher was to maintain an impersonal attitude, to explain the consequences of the child's behaviour to him or her, and to give the child the "opportunity to choose between cooperation and the consequences of non-cooperation."[37]

During play, the teachers were to manage development by providing appropriate materials and supervise development by observing continuously. However, while teachers were to be friendly and interested, they were not to lead the children's play or play with them; they were to "keep in the background; neither directing nor interfering."[38] It was argued that with a minimum of restriction and adult interference the child would learn to depend on herself and not on outside intervention. The 'best' method of interaction was with verbal suggestions or commands, and physical assistance if the former failed. "Personal" intervention, such as through encouragement or threat of discipline was considered unsatisfactory for managing child development, as "prodding, suggesting, showing ... rob the child of training inherent in doing things for oneself."[39]

The interaction style to be followed by Institute nursery school teachers was based on a respect for the child's autonomy. It was intended to counter what were considered common errors in parenting: being either too authoritarian or too protective. From the mental hygiene perspective, both styles prevented the child from achieving the independence necessary for mental health in adulthood. The former produced overly submissive children; the latter overly dependent children.

The emotional distance between teacher and child during routines was balanced by an emphasis on providing a pleasant serene atmosphere. Punishment, fear, or extrinsic reward were not used to gain children's cooperation. It was argued that this environment would make children want to cooperate in meeting "the social needs of conformity" while providing "a program which includes individual satisfaction."[40]

This form of adult-child interaction was similar to that described in early day nursery caregiving where adults were not expected to intervene in children's play, but to act in a supervisory capacity. However, the content of principles guiding this form of interaction was substantively different at the Institute's nursery school. The Institute's provision of explicit guidelines along with genetic and mental health development rationalizations identified the interactions as qualitatively different from the adult-child interactions expected within the setting of the early day nurseries. Within the normative curriculum the adult's non-participation was a means for assuming an integral role in the child's developmental progress.

When maturation theory was combined with the mental hygiene orientation, new beliefs and values were produced which made the assumption that children required a specialized form of care. Nursery schools were the social agencies intended to deliver such care. In its normative curriculum, time and space were regarded as productive of social relations. The function of the nursery was the temporal and spatial ordering of developmental time — the physical, mental and emotional chronology of the child. In the nursery school, adult-child interactions were framed by the requirement of the adult to supervise the child's developmental time. This structure provided an all encompassing and continuous organizing of children's activities while at the nursery, enabling the nursery school teachers to carry out their role as managers and supervisors of development. In these ways the curriculum of the Institute's nursery school was a radical departure from the methods of providing care for children that existed prior to its establishment. It was this model that was adopted by Canadian day nurseries.

FOOTNOTES

1 Blatz, W.E. 1926. "The St. George's School for Child Study" *University of Toronto Monthly* (June), p. 419.

2 Ross, D. 1972. *G. Stanley Hall: The Psychologist As Prophet*. Chicago: The University of Chicago Press; White, S. H. 1990. "Child Study at Clark University: 1894-1904" *Journal of the History of the Behavioral Sciences*, 26:131–150.

3 Ross, 1972, pp. 290-91. For a list of the survey topics see Lomax, E. R. with J. Kagan and B. G. Rosenkratz. 1978. *Science and Patterns of Child Care*. San Francisco: W.H. Freeman and Company, pp. 221–36.

4 Gesell, A. 1925/28. *The Mental Growth of the Pre-school Child*. NY: MacMillan.

5 Gesell, 1925/28. p. 430.

6 Richardson, T. R. 1989. *The Century of the Child: The Mental Hygiene Movement & Social Policy in the United States & Canada*. NY: State University of New York Press.

7 See Thomas, W.I. 1923/1967. *The Unadjusted Girl*. NY: Harper & Row.

8 Cohen, S. 1979. "The Mental Hygiene Movement, The Commonwealth Fund, and Public Education, 1921-1933." In G. Benjamin (Ed.), *Private Philanthropy and Public Elementary and Secondary Education*, pp. 33–46. Proceedings of the Rockefeller Archives Center Conference, June 8, p. 34.

9 Gesell, A. 1923. *The Pre-School Child: From the Standpoint of Public Hygiene and Education*, excerpts published in Gesell, 1925/28.

10 Gesell, 1925/28, pp. 11–12.

11 Gesell, A. 1924. "The Significance of the Nursery School." *Childhood Education*, 1:11–20.

12 See also Raymond, J.M. 1991. *The Nursery World of Dr. Blatz*. Toronto: University of Toronto Press.

13 Millichamp, D. 1977. Taped Interview. Pat Schulz Collection, located at the Baldwin Room, Metropolitan Toronto Reference Library, Canada.

14 BLATZ. "Annual Reports of Parent Education Division for the years 1925-26, 1926-27 and 1928"; "Analysis of Institute Population" 1961-62. Citations to BLATZ refer to archival materials in the William E. Blatz Collection, Rare Books and Special Collections Library, University of Toronto, Canada.

15 Blatz, W.E., Millichamp, D., & Fletcher, M. 1935. *Nursery Education: Theory and Practice.* NY: William Morrow and Company, pp. 21–22.

16 See also Varga, D. 1993. "From a Service for Mothers to the Developmental Management of Children: Day Nursery Care in Canada, 1890-1960." *Advances in Early Education and Day Care,* In S. Reifal (Ed.), 5:113–141. Connecticut: Jai press.

17 Blatz, W.E. 1944. *Understanding the Young Child.* Toronto: Clarke,Irwin & Company Limited.

18 Blatz, W.E. & Bott, H. 1930. *The Management of Young Children.* NY: William Morrow & Company, p. 13–14. Emphasis in original.

19 Blatz et. al. 1935, pp. 23–27.

20 BLATZ. Minutes of Staff Meeting, December 1, 1926.

21 Blatz et. al. 1935, pp. 24–25.

22 Blatz et. al. 1935, p. 44.

23 Blatz et. al. 1935, pp. 148–49.

24 *Parent Education Bulletin* No.4 (1939):7.

25 Blatz, 1944, p. 246.

26 Varga, D. 1991. "The Historical Ordering of Children's Play as a Developmental Task." *Play & Culture* 4:322–333.

27 Blatz et. al. 1935, p. 159.

28 Adler, L. M. 1928. "Record Keeping." *Childhood Education,* 4:362.

29 Blatz et. al. 1935, p. 169.

30 BLATZ. "The Saga of William Emet Blatz, Part III" by Mary J. Wright, 1985.

31 Blatz et. al. 1935, pp. 47–48.

32 Blatz et. al. 1935, p. 50.

33 Blatz et. al. 1935. p. 47–48.

34 Blatz et al. 1935, p. 48.

35 Millichamp, 1977. Interview.

36 Blatz et. al. 1935, p. 39.

37 Blatz et. al. 1935, p. 46.

38 Blatz et. al. 1935, p. 168.

39 Blatz et. al. 1935, p. 37 and p. 169; Blatz and Bott. 1930, p. 122.

40 Blatz et al. 1935, p. 19.

Chapter Four

Writing, Talking and Teaching about the New Child

> You have to show the link to nursery education. The education program was the base of all future developments in day care and nursery school. [We were] very lucky, there weren't a lot of them [day nurseries] so didn't have a lot to change. All the ones added that were recognized had this initial background.[1]

As the major child study research centre in Canada until the 1950s, the Institute held a central role in the production of knowledge about children. William Blatz was the dominant voice of the Institute. From 1925 to 1960, it was his vision of childhood that was carried on in the work of the Institute and beyond its doors through such dissemination activities as lecturing, writing, participating in associations, teacher training, and policy making.

Dorothy Millichamp, quoted above, has expressed the profound influence these activities had on day nursery child care. This chapter describes the processes by which the ideas of the Institute's nursery school child care curriculum were made known to others. It does not outline all the outreach activities of Institute faculty, but focuses primarily on the links established through dissemination, between the Institute and day nurseries.

Publicization

Publicization, the writing and talking about child study knowledge, maturation theory, and mental hygiene principles, was a method of informing others of the ideas implemented in the Institute's nursery school curriculum. From the 1920s to the 1950s, the ideas and practices of Blatz and other Institute members were disseminated in great quantity, to a variety of audiences, and through various media. These included appearances at conferences and public lectures; writings in academic, professional and popular publications; broadcasts of radio and television programs.

Blatz lectured in every capital and secondary city in Canada west of Ontario. In the United States, he lectured on the eastern seaboard, throughout the mid-west and on the west coast. In 1940 and 1941, he gave lectures and short courses throughout England and in Scotland. He spoke at academic conferences including the Canadian National Committee for Mental Hygiene, the Fifth International Congress on Mental Health, and both the Canadian and American Psychology Associations. He gave talks to parents at such meetings as the Women's City Club in Cleveland Ohio, and the Annual Meeting of Parents' Council of Philadelphia. He also lectured for nurses and teachers such as at the Chicago Institute for Teaching and the Birmingham Association of the National Union of Teachers.

Blatz's eighty-three speaking engagements just for the one year period of 1955-56, provide a sense of the exposure his ideas received through this type of publicization. Sixty talks were to various home and school associations, six were to nursery school parent groups, six were to nursery school and kindergarten teacher groups or associations, and eleven were to education associations and boards of education.

Blatz also gave radio talks and made numerous television appearances, particularly as a guest on the Canadian Broadcasting Corporation debate program "Fighting Words." Such activities allowed for the presentation of his ideas through a popular public venue and probably assisted in establishing him as a professional celebrity.[2] The radio and television broadcasts included discussions about childhood, education, and child rearing practices. The titles of three broadcasts provide an indication of the concerns addressed by Blatz: "Should Parents Bring Up Children," "What's Wrong with our Educational System," and at the end of the second world war, "The Soldier's Return to His Children."

While speaking engagements provide the opportunity to present ideas to an audience, in the immediate sense they are typically a one-way communication process of short duration. By contrast, involvement in associations allows for the possibility of the permeation of ideas into a broader base of activities. Associations are the "major formal means by which the interests of its members are expressed collectively and focused politically."[3] The membership of Blatz and other Institute staff in academic, professional, government, and community associations increased their audience and the potential influence of their ideas. In 1953 alone, Institute staff participated in fifty associations that included local, provincial, national and international organizations.[4] Professional societies with Institute members were various education associations, nursery associations, the National Vocational Guidance Association (USA), and the Canadian Camping Association. Government groups included the Toronto Family Court, the Toronto Board of Education, and the National Research Council. Teaching associations included the Red Cross Homemaker's Course, the Hospital for Sick Children, the Faculty of Household Science (University of Toronto). Of particular interest — because it demonstrates their involvement in post-secondary teaching beyond the Institute — was the inclusion of Institute members in two Ryerson Polytechnic teaching groups. Community groups included the Canada Welfare Council, the Ontario Federation of Home and Schools, and the Ontario Children's Aid and Infants' Homes.

Another form of publicization was through writing. Blatz was perhaps the most prolific of Institute's faculty in this regard. He provided regular contributions to the Institute's in-house publications. One of these was *Child Study Pamphlets*, which provided detailed reports of Institute research. The other was *Parent Education Bulletin*, established in 1938 to consolidate the research and parent-education functions of the Institute. It included articles on child training, reviews of books and articles, lists of child-welfare services and activities, and recommendations for further readings. Its subscription list of "parents, workers in nursery and parent education, psychologists, teachers of older children, professionals in other and allied fields such as medicine, nursing, social work and religion"[5] ensured the ideas presented through the *Bulletin* reached a diverse readership.

Beyond these writings, Blatz authored at least eighty publications, covering a wide range of topics and intended for a variety of audiences including parents, child care practitioners, teachers, and child study researchers. He was the principal author of five books, and the second author of *We Go To Nursery School*, a photograph book written for parents and children as an introduction to the routine of the nursery school. He contributed chapters to books and academic articles to journals such as *Child Study*, *Pedagogical Seminary*, *Genetic Psychology Monographs*, *Canadian Journal of Psychology*, and the *Canadian Psychology Association Bulletin*. From 1944 to 1947, he wrote a monthly child rearing column for the popular magazine, *Chatelaine*. His writings for professional publications were featured mostly in *Child Welfare Pamphlets*, and the *Journal of the National Education Association*.

Reviews of Blatz's books in the popular press as well as in professional and academic journals made it unnecessary for people to read the books in order to be aware of his ideas. Positive reviews, especially by other child care experts, gave credence and status to the work. An example was Blatz and Bott's *Parents and Preschool Children* being awarded *Parents' Magazine* annual medal for best parent's book of 1928. Another was a review in *Parents' Magazine* of that book by the behaviourist John B. Watson. It read in part:

> It is so sanely and so clearly written. The material is very, very good and the attitude of the authors is beyond criticism. I do hope it will have a wide sale to mothers all over this country. Of all the books which have been coming out on children the last few years, I think this is the best.[6]

Media coverage of Blatz and his ideas of child care was another source of popular publicization. In the mid-1930s he was the focus of such attention due to his role in managing the preschool care of the Dionne quintuplets. Publicization also took place through newspaper coverage of Blatz's lectures at public and professional meetings. This suggests widespread public interest in what he had to say. As with book reviews, even when these were negative they extended Blatz's audience from those in attendance at the meetings to those who read the newspaper articles. The newspaper coverage also provided recognition of Blatz as a controversial expert in matters of the child. A lecture by Blatz during which he criticised parents' child rearing abilities and urged mandatory nursery school education was reported with reactions of various community leaders:

> Trustee Mrs. Groves strongly believed in the good influence of the parents on the child. "It would be a very serious thing if the affection of the parents were eliminated in the upbringing of the child," she said. "In my opinion the parents do count and count materially. I am a strong believer in the precepts and love of parents and it would be a sad day when the child is taken from its parents." ... Reverend J. Phillips Jones, secretary of the Social Service Council of Canada, held similar views. "I know that Dr. Blatz is very advanced in his ideas," he said, "he has made a big study of the question and his own views, but I would not care to endorse all he says."[7]

Another article designated Blatz "a blot on modern society" for criticizing marriage as an institution.[8] When Blatz urged educators to emphasize culture rather than mathematics and reading, and expressed his opposition to the Boy Scout movement, an editor remarked:

> Psychology, which is the science of the nature, functions, and phenomena of the human soul and mind, admits of a lot of abuse and a lot of hokum, and that as much as we have a right to believe in it there is need to be careful about certain psychologists.[9]

Newspaper stories about Institute courses and its nursery school was further publicization of the maturation and mental hygiene ideas. Articles about the courses sometimes simply listed what was being offered, but others provided detailed descriptions of content by a reporter who enrolled in them.[10] The articles about the nursery school described its daily routine and philosophy of child care. In some cases, these stories were closely controlled by the Institute, as when a reporter was given permission to visit the nursery school only if the article was submitted for review before publication.[11] While much was reported in Toronto newspapers about the curriculum of the Institute's nursery school, there seems to have been little critical comment about its form of child care. The only negative review found was of the nursery school routines described in the Institute's textbook for nursery school teachers:

> Anyone who wants a definite guide for training children efficiently during the pre-school era should find the detailed "routines" which are here described invaluable — and also, it is to be feared, rather formidable. For the professional infant educators do take their work so seriously and conduct it in such a complicated fashion.... Surely in the matter of thoroughness and tediousness, the mechanics of nursery education have surpassed all other types of pedagogy.[12]

Despite the wide-spread media criticism of Blatz and his ideas, and the questioning of the appropriateness of mothers leaving young children in the care of others, the Institute model of nursery school child care was largely praised and most of the stories about the nursery school marvelled at the children's independence and good behaviour.

While it is not known how publicization specifically influenced persons involved with the early day nurseries, undoubtedly it was an important feature in the broader social context whereby the ideas of Institute faculty, especially as expressed by Blatz, attained dominance over competing beliefs and values about children and their care.

Normalization

Publicization of the Institute's nursery school curriculum contributed to its acceptance as a model for day nursery caregiving. However, the Institute's provision of graduate programs in child study, and training programs for nursery school teachers and day nursery workers probably had the most direct impact on transforming the early day nurseries, and establishing the practices and policies of the more recent nurseries. The normalization of caregiving practices, that is, making practices standard through training, enabled the ideas of the Institute to be put into practice. A vast array of normalization activities was undertaken by the Institute. Those most directly related to day nursery caregiving were its graduate program of psychology, and its nursery training courses.

The Institute's courses followed the social engineering pattern of training teachers for formal schooling. Informed by relations of power and social structures, teacher training is a historically developed and transmitted method of classifying and regulating teachers. The structural features of teacher training reinforces the culturally dominant traditions of educational institutions. This is achieved through the presentation of expert knowledge in lectures, student observation of methods modelled by experts, and the supervision of students' practical work by faculty.[13] More than ensuring that students are knowledgable about what constitutes good teaching, it formulates an understanding of what it means to be a good teacher.

The nursery school was at the centre of the Institute's normalization process, for it was used as a model of normative caregiving and it was there that students carried out practical work under the supervision of its faculty. From the opening years of the Institute, day nursery caregivers enrolled in its special lectures for professionals, took courses from the graduate program, and undertook practise teaching in its nursery school. Graduates from the Institute's psychology degree program became nursery directors. In 1941 the Institute offered a two year course for nursery school supervisors. This was Canada's first specialized nursery school training course.

An increased demand for nursery caregivers arose with the establishment of wartime day nurseries during the second world war.[14] Funded by the federal government, the nurseries made it possible for mothers with young children to enter the paid labour force, and thereby ease the shortage of workers created by the demands of war. Twenty-eight wartime nurseries operated in Ontario and five in Quebec, providing care for children between the ages of two and six. At first, volunteers had been expected to provide the bulk of the caregiving labour. However, according to Dorothy Millichamp, Assistant Director of the Institute during the 1940s, the volunteer's lack of formal child study and nursery school training soon made the nurseries "unworkable."[15]

The Institute was at the forefront of creating training programs for the influx of nursery caregivers. It shortened its two year diploma course to nine months, and in 1942, also offered a nine-week course for volunteers.[16] The Institute was also responsible for establishing, in October 1942, the Provincial Day Nursery Training Centre. Located in Toronto, the Training Centre was directed and staffed by graduates of the Institute of Child Study, and its program followed the Institute's nursery school curriculum. It provided supervised practical work, with the intention of ensuring "that the programme in each nursery may incorporate the same principles of nursery education."[17] In 1945 a short training course was offered by the Institute for new high school graduates to train as junior assistants in the wartime nurseries.[18]

The Training Centre and the Institute's day nursery courses were terminated in 1946, when the wartime day nurseries were closed due to a withdrawal of federal funding. However, the impact of these courses was long-term because of the influence their graduates had on the day nursery field. Mary Northway, an Institute faculty member, has remarked that the wartime day nurseries provided a "tradition to grow on," as the caregivers trained during this period "stayed in the field to retirement."[19] The nursery graduates of the 1940s courses became extremely influential in the regulation of day nursery practices and policies. They became leaders of the Nursery Education Association of Ontario, established in February 1946 (later the Association for Early Childhood Education, Ontario). Through this association the graduates established a number of training programs in Ontario during the 1970s, and an accreditation system for day nursery workers in the 1980s.

Regulation

Through publicization and normalization activities, Institute members were able to extend their ideas and practices beyond the Institute's nursery school, and into the day nurseries and the practices of caregivers. A third component in the process of transforming day nurseries was legal regulation, by which the normative curriculum of the Institute's nursery school became the required standard for Ontario day nurseries to follow. Regulation was achieved in two phases. In the first phase the Institute established guidelines for the Ontario wartime day nurseries; in the second phase it produced legal standards for all Ontario day nurseries.

Canada, unlike some other countries such as Japan and China, has no history of nationally regulating the form of care provided by day nurseries.[20] Prior to the mid-1940s, Canadian day nursery practices were decided upon by the persons who organized the agencies and who acted on their boards of directors. The only state regulation of these early nurseries was through municipal fire safety requirements. The first government involvement in caregiving practices occurred with the 1943 Dominion-Provincial Agreement for Wartime Day Nurseries, whereby the provinces were given responsibility for their establishment and operation. Ontario was the only province to actually develop nursery regulations under this Agreement. The regulations for wartime day nursery caregiving practices were created by Institute faculty. Except for an extended day, the procedures of its nursery school were replicated.[21] A Provincial Advisory Committee, headed by Mary Blakslee, a graduate of the Institute of Child Study and supervisor of the West End Creche, oversaw their implementation. Each city and town had to appoint a Local Committee, which drew up plans for providing nurseries, and, after approval by the Provincial Committee, to administer them.[22] Dorothy Millichamp was seconded from the Institute to act as supervisor and advisor for the Toronto Committee.

In 1943, the Provincial Advisory Committee was subsumed under the umbrella provincial department of Public Health and Welfare and was renamed the Division of Wartime Day Nurseries and Day Care. At this time, Millichamp was appointed Director of the Wartime Nurseries Division while still retaining her Institute position.[23] As Director of this provincial agency, Millichamp had the responsibility of visiting the nurseries and providing advice and information to ensure that practices followed the guidelines.[24] There were no legal penalties for not complying with the guidelines, and funding was the primary means for inducing nurseries to follow them.[25] For example, the West End Creche had to hire an additional trained worker and renovate its playground before it received financial aid as a wartime day nursery (for providing care for kindergarten children).[26]

When the federal government withdrew its funding for day nurseries at the end of the war, the Ontario provincial government was inundated with requests from mothers to keep them operating, and from day nursery directors and organizers to regulate them through licensing procedures. Dorothy Millichamp played a key role in the outcome. As head of the Division of Wartime Day Nurseries and Day Care, Millichamp was expected to maintain a neutral position with regard to both funding and licensing. However, she was involved in the parent's fight for the continuation of the nurseries.[27] At the same time, she publicly stated that while day nurseries should be available to "poor families," they should not be available for all children.[28] She argued against day nursery care in general, contending that the long hours and monotony of caring for children took tremendous effort, with people tending "to get careless," thereby putting children at risk.[29] The government decision was to withdraw funding from the wartime day nurseries, to fund the previously established nurseries, and to regulate all day nurseries through provincial legislation.

In 1946 the Government of Ontario requested Institute faculty to create the guidelines for the legislation, indicating the status of expertise that the Institute held over matters of child care. William Blatz, Dorothy Millichamp and Mary Northway took on this task.[30] In outlining the organization of space, and the equipment needed, they replicated the structure and materials of the Institute nursery school. Furthermore, they specified that the daily program was to "conform to standards currently accepted by the Institute of Child Study of the University of Toronto."[31] These guidelines became the basis of the Ontario Day Nurseries Act of 1946; they required all day nurseries in the province to follow the Institute child care curriculum. The mandate that the Institute program be followed remained part of the Act until a 1968 revision. While this legislation was only applicable to Ontario programs, it was used to guide subsequent nursery regulations in other provinces, increasing the Institute's influence throughout the day nurseries of Canada. Lois Evans, on the board of directors for the Winnipeg Day Nursery, wrote in response to changes being undertaken at that nursery that "as we have no Nursery School legislation in Manitoba, that of Ontario has been used as a pattern."[32] In addition to specifying the curriculum of day nurseries, the Act established the requirements that nursery directors had to have some formal knowledge about children's development.[33]

The Ontario Day Nurseries Branch was created to license and supervise nursery practices. Once again, Institute influence was present, this time in the person of the Branch's first Director, Elsie Stapleford, an Institute graduate. Under the terms of the Act, current nurseries and those thereafter established had to receive a Day Nursery License in order to operate legally. The licensing procedure required the submission of a written application, setting out a description of the nursery facilities, the age and number of children to be cared for, and the type of program that would be carried out. Applications were expected to adhere to the Day Nursery regulations based on the Institute nursery school program. Field supervisors were to visit the nurseries to ensure all regulations were being followed. Licenses were good for one year; re-licensing required the resubmission of documentation as well as the approval of the field supervisors.

The primary inducement for complying with the guidelines was provincial funding. If this failed to gain cooperation, the nurseries were coerced into compliance by the threat of having their licenses withdrawn. However, it appears that this measure was rarely imposed. In the months prior to the Act coming into effect, most nurseries were undertaking procedures to be licensed. It was reported that by March 31st, 1947, 145 nurseries had applied for a licence; fourteen others had recently been notified of the regulations, but had not yet returned their applications; 134 had been visited by field supervisors; sixty-one of these had been issued a license; fifty-five others qualified, except for municipal requirements [generally fire regulations, perceived by Branch officials to be a matter of technical improvement]; eighteen "were endeavouring to make the necessary adjustments to meet the standards as set forth in the Regulations." In 1948-49, only five of ninety unlicensed nurseries were "not trying to get licensed." For the year 1949-50, it was noted that "of 81 unlicensed nurseries only nine are making no progress towards securing a license."[34] It is likely that legal regulation was achieved fairly easily because the publicization and normalization activities of the Institute had created a climate whereby the leaders in the day nursery field held ideas that corresponded to those set out in the Act.

In this chapter the multiple activities engaged in by Institute members to change beliefs and values about children and their care have been described. Publications, public speaking, membership in associations, newspaper stories, education of caregivers, creation of legal standards, and holding government positions were the means by which the ideas of the Institute nursery's normative child care curriculum were disseminated beyond the Institute to provincial, national and international audiences. Included in these audiences were day nursery caregivers. The following chapter sets out the impact this had on Canada's earliest day nurseries.

FOOTNOTES

1 Millichamp, 1977. Interview.
2 See also Varga, D. 1996. "Communicating the Authority of Child Care Expertise: Canada's *School for Parents* 1942-1960." *Women's Studies in Communication*, forthcoming.
3 Freidson, E. 1986. *Professional Powers: A Study of the Institutionalization of Formal Knowledge*. Chicago: The University of Chicago Press, p. 186.
4 BLATZ. January, 1953.
5 BLATZ. "Annual Report of the ICS, 1955-56."
6 BLATZ. Book Reviews 1927-1943. For a discussion of the key place of *Parents' Magazine* in the history of child rearing ideas see Schlossman, S. 1985. "Perils of Popularization: The Founding of *Parents' Magazine*." In A. Boardman Smuts & J.W. Hagen (Eds.), *History and Research in Child Development*, Monographs of the Society for Research in Child Development, *50* (4–5, Serial No. 211):65–77.
7 BLATZ. "Parents Need Training More than Children" *Toronto Star*, September 1930.
8 "Dr. Blatz is a 'Blot' on Modern Society" *Toronto Star*, May 16, 1934.
9 "Teaching the New Child" *Ottawa Journal*, May 3, 1935.
10 BLATZ. "Mother Visits Nursery School." newspaper articles, c. early 1930s.
11 BLATZ. Minutes, October 29, 1926.
12 [Untitled Review of Blatz et al. 1935] *New York Herald Tribune Books*, December 1, 1935.
13 See Varga, D. 1991. "Neutral and Timeless Truths: An Historical Analy-

sis of Observation and Evaluation in Teacher Training." *The Journal of Educational Thought 25*(1):12–26.

14 See also Pierson, R. R. 1986 *"They're Still Women After All": The Second World War and Canadian Womanhood.* Toronto: McClelland & Stewart.

15 Millichamp, 1977. Interview.

16 Northway, M. L. 1977. Taped interview. Pat Schulz Collection, located at the Baldwin Room, Metropolitan Toronto Reference Library, Canada.

17 *Parent Education Bulletin* No. 24 (1943):11.

18 *Parent Education Bulletin* No.32 (1945):9.

19 Northway, 1977. Interview.

20 See Feeney, S. 1992. *Early Childhood Education in Asia and the Pacific: A Source Book.* NY: Garland Publishing.

21 BLATZ. "Minimum Requirements and Approximate Expenditures for a Nursery School with an Attendance of 30 children," 1942.

22 *Parent Education Bulletin* No.19 (1942):19.

23 "Given High Post in Nursery Work" *Globe and Mail*, November 10, 1943.

24 Millichamp, 1977. Interview.

25 No Author. 1942. "Dominion-Provincial Agreement on Day Nurseries." *Canadian Welfare, 18*(3):11–12.

26 WEC. President's Report, 1945.

27 Millichamp, 1977. Interview. For a discussion of the role of the parent committee in this struggle see Prentice, S. 1989. "Workers, Mothers, Reds: Toronto's Postwar Daycare Fight." *Studies in Political Economy, 30*:115–141.

28 BLATZ. "Big Adjustment Foreseen for Women Following War" newspaper article c. January, 1944.

29 Millichamp, 1977. Interview.

30 Northway, M. 1973. "Child Study in Canada: A Casual History." In L. M. Brockman, J. H. Whitely, & J. P. Zubek (Eds.), *Child Development: Selected Readings.* Toronto: McClelland & Stewart, pp. 11–45.

31 Ontario, "Regulations Made Under The Day Nurseries Act," 1950. Printed in the 1950 Ontario Statutes, these were the regulations of the 1946 Act.

32 WDN. Letter from Lois Evans to J.M. Sinclair, Chairman, The Community Chest, December 8, 1953.

33 For a detailed discussion of Canadian regulations governing day nursery training requirements see Varga, D. Forthcoming. "History of Teacher Education." In L. Prochner & N. Howe (Eds.), *Early Childhood Care and Education in Canada: Past, Present, and Future.* BC: University of British Columbia Press.

34 Day Nurseries Branch, Annual Reports for 1947, 1948-49, and 1949-50. Pat Schulz Collection, located at the Baldwin Room, Metropolitan Toronto Reference Library, Canada.

Chapter Five

Transformation of Canadian Day Nurseries

There has been a vast change in operations of the centre. For years, it was simply a custodial-care building which served as a relief place for mothers.... Thinking has changed with the times. Now, the centre thinks primarily of the children.[1]

Canada's earliest day nurseries began to change their practices of child care after 1925. Their social roles, organization of caregiving time, space, and interactions, and use of observation were transformed in accordance with the normative curriculum as modeled primarily by the Institute's nursery school. Change did not occur evenly for all the nurseries. The 1925 division is only a frame of reference, not a line marking the complete end of one form of care and the absolute beginning of another. Some aspects of care did not change until much later than 1925, but that year does mark a definite beginning of the transformation of beliefs and values about Canadian day nursery caregiving. As the quote at the beginning of this chapter suggests, not only had practices changed, but so had ideas of what was considered good care, and therefore the reasons for the existence of the nurseries. This transformation is illustrated through the changes that took place at the same day nurseries discussed in chapter two.

Social Roles of the Nurseries

The central principle guiding the transformation in the practices of the day nurseries was the shift away from their social role of providing employment and child care so that mothers could work in order to support their families. In carrying out that earlier role, a variety of services were components of the day nursery agencies, such as ensuring the children, and sometimes their families, received medical care, food, milk, and clothing. From the mid-1920s, this social service role declined as the nurseries increasingly adopted the role of supervising and managing children's genetic and personality development. While the nurseries continued to act as employment agencies until the mid-1940s, this became a secondary function. After the Second World War, the nurseries stopped their employment services, and many also curtailed much of their charitable community work. This is not to say that individual nursery members did not carry on community activities. Some were extensively involved in other aspects of social services, but such work no longer was regarded as an essential role of day nurseries.

Persons involved with the nurseries identified the social role

Ottawa Day Nursery 1936 "Kindergarten Room."

change as evidence of a move from poor to good care. The director of the Winnipeg nursery remarked, "The old nurseries, dating back to 1909 in Winnipeg, provided only custodial care but the modern nursery is concerned with mental, emotional and social development as well as physical care."[2] The following passage from 1962 Annual Report of the Ottawa nursery exemplifies how this changed role resulted in a negative interpretation of prior practices.

> The Nursery was a catch-all for every situation from abandonment to unplaceable children. Mrs. Fleming recalls one girl, Annie, who spent her winters here because her mother's home was not warm enough and no one seemed prepared to take the girl on. She was 14, of limited intelligence and loved to pound the piano with one finger. This got on everyone's nerves until one night she was told to stop, whereupon she took scissors, went to a cupboard and cut one of the staff's dresses to ribbons. The Nursery no longer takes on this kind of responsibility, and no one would think of asking us to....
>
> The nature of our service has changed — it is not the staff doing for the mothers and children, but parents and Nursery participating in the placement of the children with a particular aim in mind.[3]

The particular 'aim' referred to, was the management and supervision of genetic and mental health development.

Caregiver Characteristics

With the transformation of the role of the nurseries, more caregiving staff were hired. Although untrained workers remained the majority of employees within the nurseries, specialized child development training was acknowledged as essential in order for the nurseries to fulfil their role of supervising and managing children's development. The nurseries appear to have hired trained workers when they were available.

For most of the agencies, the first employees to be hired with specialized training where the directors. Institute graduate Marjorie Burgess became the director of the West End Creche in 1928. She left the next year, and was replaced by another Institute graduate, Gretta Gordon, who remained director for eight years. When she left, she was replaced by Margaret Lovatt, who had social work and Institute training. She remained director until the 1960s. Margaret Twitchell, also an Institute graduate, became the director of the East End Day Nursery in 1938, where she remained until its closure in 1959. Elma Nelson, who had nursery school training (but it is unclear from where) was hired by the Ottawa Day Nursery in 1948. When Nelson left in 1949 to be married, she was replaced by Mary Laing, a graduate of the Institute's war time nursery training program. She remained its director for thirteen years. At the Winnipeg nursery in 1953 Gretta Brown (nee Gordon, who had directed the West End Creche) was hired as director, a position she held until her retirement, in 1976.

Caregivers with nursery school training were also desirable employees. In 1929 Victoria Day Nursery added a nursery school teacher to its staff of six untrained workers. Also in 1929, the West End Creche hired two workers who had attended the Institute's nursery school lectures and who had carried out practical work supervised by Institute faculty. In 1948, at the Montreal nursery "a nursery school supervisor (who could teach the staff modern methods of child care) and one additional nursery school teacher were added to the staff."[4] In 1950 Annie Thexton, who had taken a course in child study from the Merrill Palmer School in the United States, was hired at the Winnipeg Day Nursery. By 1953 the Victoria nursery employed a nursery school supervisor, and six assistants with different levels of training.[5]

The organizers of the Montreal nursery complained that the absence of child study training in that city made it difficult for them to find trained staff. To compensate for this, the organizers paid the expenses of some of their nursery staff to attend Toronto Institute summer programs. This included a Miss O'Neill who took the Basic Nursery School Education course, and a Miss MacNeil who took a post-graduate course in Art for the Preschool Child. In addition, some of the caregivers attended courses at the Eliot Pearson Nursery Training School at Tufts University, Boston. Since the 1950s, Winnipeg and Ottawa nursery caregivers also attended short summer courses at the Toronto Institute. The Winnipeg nursery was occasionally able to hire women who had studied child development in U.S. colleges or universities. The importance of having trained workers was highlighted by the

Montreal nursery organizers, who remarked:

> Courses and monthly lectures cannot take the place of concentrated and intensive training of one or more years.... It is our duty to see that the teacher who is responsible for the preschool child in his most impressionable years, should have the best that we can offer him in Nursery School Training and experience.[6]

Gretta Brown stated, "It is important that those working with him [the preschool child] have a knowledge of child development and sensitivity to the total needs of the child and his family."[7] Likewise, the emphasis on hiring trained caregivers at the East End nursery was explained as a positive change, "from untrained, sometimes rather ignorant nursemaids, to a trained nursery school worker, with assistants capable of being directed along proper lines."[8] "Proper lines" referred to the normative curriculum.

There is little information available that describes desirable caregiving characteristics beyond specialized training. It would be expected that the same characteristics recommended for nursery school teachers by the Toronto Institute were preferred. However, for at least the Montreal Day Nursery in the mid 1940s, the Institute's recommendation of detached adult-child interactions were eschewed for "close, satisfying, affectionate relationships" between children and caregivers.[9] The director of that nursery in 1960 noted the importance of caregivers being motherly in their orientation toward children. Day nursery staff were "not only to provide an interesting programme for these children, but also to be a substitute mother, to listen to, and console the child who has had a bad day, ... and to share the enthusiasm of the youngster who is beginning to find out the joys of learning."[10]

In addition to caregivers with nursery school training, social workers took up positions of leadership in the nurseries. In the 1940s, the Montreal Day Nursery had a social worker on staff and the West End Creche was supervised by a social worker. By 1953 Victoria Day Nursery had two social workers on its staff and was classified by the Ontario government as a demonstration centre for testing out the feasibility of running a day nursery with social worker staff and with a casework committee responsible for policy. Although social work values were an important aspect of day nursery care until the 1960s, the influence of these professionals was largely in the area of nursery-parent relations. They determined who received care and referred children and parents to other social services when necessary.

Associated with the employment of trained staff was a change in the roles of the caregivers and organizers. Those trained in child study or nursery school methods were acknowledged by the organizers as experts in the care of children. As discussed in Chapter Two, prior to the implementation of the normative curriculum, adult roles in the nurseries were primarily geared toward maintaining the physical health of children and supervising children's moral conduct. With the hiring of trained caregivers the focus changed to managing and supervising children's development. A key aspect of this change in caregiving roles was a reorganization of day nursery labour. In the early years of the day nurseries, caregivers where responsible for both the care of the children and housekeeping tasks. After the mid-1920s, caregiving labour was confined to child care tasks, and domestic staff were limited to housekeeping duties. This was formalized through job titles, such as at the Ottawa Day Nursery where it was reported that "Mrs. Nelson lists her staff under 2 headings, Nursery School and Household."[11] The previous lack of division of labour came to be considered problematic. According to the 1953 minutes of the Winnipeg Day Nursery: "Previously a great deal of use was made of a kitchen maid living in. Staff were responsible for a great many duties in connection with the running of the nursery. My feeling is that it has been quite unsatisfactory."[12]

In addition to this division of labour, the caregivers' responsibility for defining the curriculum of the nurseries increased. An example of the greater authority of trained caregivers is found in the following excerpt from the 1945 minutes of the West End Creche:

> Mrs. Sowter returned to the Creche fresh from six weeks training course with ideas of changing the Department, so that even though many of the children are younger than two on admission, their daily programme would be planned along nursery school lines.... Mrs. Sowter has reorganized the Department until it is now a "full-fledged" Junior Nursery School.[13]

Ottawa Day Nursery 1937–38 "Toddlers' Dining Room." The kidney shaped
table was intended to allow a caregiver to be seated in the centre,
where she could observe all the children as they ate.

In contrast to the meetings of the early day nursery organizers,
the 1940s board meetings included substantial reports on the
work of the caregivers, and the nursery directors were included
in discussions of the agencies' child care practices and policies. In 1966 at the Ottawa nursery, the increased participation
of the caregivers in the administration of that agency was considered important enough to be remarked upon:

> While in the past it was necessary for this [case study] commit-
> tee to be available to the staff to discuss and give advice on
> many details, we are now faced with a change of role. It is the
> staff who must lead us and educate us in the needs of the agen-
> cy and to help us in making decisions necessary to the develop-
> ment of its optimum potential.[14]

The history of the Winnipeg nursery demonstrates that those
with specialized training, especially from the Toronto Institute,
were given the authority to shape nursery practices. In 1939, at
the request of the Federated Budget Board (later the Community Chest, later the United Way) a study of the nursery was car-

ried out by Nan Ord, a graduate of the Institute's nursery school program. She reported the "premises, facilities, equipment, program and health provision" as being "below standard."[15] Since there were no formal nursery guidelines in Manitoba at that time, the standards she was referring to were likely the practices of the Institute's nursery school. In 1947, Idell Robinson, a graduate of the Institute and director of her own nursery school, was requested by Winnipeg public health officials to review the Winnipeg nursery. Her report "mentioned evident drawbacks in the physical facilities and criticized the program. She placed the blame largely on the fact there was not sufficient staff or trained personnel working with the children."[16] Apparently some changes were made in response to this report, including the hiring in 1950 of Annie Thexton, as nursery school supervisor. In 1953, Gretta Brown was asked to carry out another study of the nursery, after which she became its director and reorganized its practices explicitly using the nursery school of her alma mater, the Toronto Institute, as its model.[17]

Specialized training of caregivers provided the day nurseries with personnel who held knowledge, beliefs and values about child care that were based on the normative curriculum. Nursery organizers came to view these as essential caregiving characteristics. Along with the changed role of staff in the nurseries, changes were made in the organization of caregiving policies and practices.

Transformation of Day Nursery Caregiving

Prior to the 1920s, the day nursery organization of child care practices was largely continuous with the patterns of the larger social system, that is, time and space were organized around the carrying out of specific activities required for the functioning of the institution. This included adult oriented tasks of preparing food, feeding the children, doing laundry and other housekeeping. Children's activities that took place outside the time and space of these necessary tasks, such as playing, sleeping, and toileting were considered personal activities, and therefore not requiring adult intervention beyond necessary physical assistance. Since the 1920s, both adult oriented tasks and children's personal activities were redefined as being open to, and requiring, developmental supervision and management; personal activities were thereby converted into institutional activities.

Initially, this conversion was carried out through the provision of what was referred to as 'habit training'; the establishment of routines in everyday behaviours. The East End Day Nursery established a habit school in 1931; in the 1930s, the West End Creche reported habit training as their main focus; "The primary objects of our work with the children are to train the child in the fundamental habits, to assist him in his development so that the attributes of initiative, self-reliance, confidence and sociability may be his by nature."[18] By the 1940s the day nursery habit schools had been superseded by nursery school departments. At the Victoria and East End agencies, nursery schools were originally established separate from their day nursery programs, but by the late 1940s, the nursery school normative curriculum was fully incorporated into day nursery care.

Transformation of Day Nursery Temporal Structures

In their adoption of the normative curriculum, the nurseries studied here underwent major changes in the areas of institutional time: routines, ages cared for, grouping of children, and attendance policies. The Institute's nursery school timetable provided the temporal model for the day nurseries' management of development. By the 1930s, the timetable of the East End nursery set out that children arrived at 7 a.m., had breakfast at 8:00, went outside for 1 1/2 hours, came in at 10:30 "to wash their face and hands, put on slippers and set about drinking milk or prune juice," had indoor play, then a "circle time, then a short rest, lunch, afternoon nap, wash up, then outside play."[19] The other Toronto nurseries had similar schedules in the 1930s, and by the 1950s so did those in Montreal, Ottawa, and Winnipeg. A description of the Montreal nursery schedule reveals its similarity to both the form and content of the Institutes' nursery school:

> A typical day at the nursery runs as follows: the child[ren] come at eight and plays for two hours in the playroom ... or in the playground if the weather is fine; at ten ... [they] have milk and cookies, then they go to the playroom for about an hour. Lunch follows.... A long sleeping period follows, then a serving of

fruit juice or milk, then play, and later in the afternoon talks, stories and music. Supper is served between 4:30 and five.[20]

The reason for organizing the children's entire day within temporal guidelines was not related to efficiency. Rather, it was viewed as essential for the developmental and mental hygiene opportunities it offered the child: "The child participates in a program designed for his age which include toilet training, elementary hygiene, games, constructive work, singing, etc., a routine that is planned to assist him to develop his faculties, and to become a member of a social group."[21]

There are indications that the temporal routines of the normative curriculum were not blindly adopted, but were modified to suit the particular reality of the day nurseries. At the East End nursery, the director explained the situation:

> Like the day of the housekeeper at home the day of the nursery worker is made up of interruptions. You may plan a routine as carefully as possible, but when half-a-dozen children come in at noon with wet feet, or someone comes in from school with a sore throat and a rash or a child cuts his head open, the routine must go while time is taken to find dry stockings, or call a doctor, or go to the hospital.[22]

In addition to incorporating the normative organization of routines into day nursery practice, the nurseries also underwent a transformation in philosophies and practices regarding the ages of children for whom care was provided. Between 1930 and 1960 at all the nurseries studied here, infant and school age care were gradually eliminated until, with the occasional exception, only preschool and kindergarten-aged children were accepted. The rationale for this change was a combination of both maturationist and mental hygiene arguments about developmental readiness of children for the social experience of nurseries. In addition, the ideas of John Bowlby about the developmental dangers faced by the young cared for by persons other than their mothers, were cited as reasons.[23]

At the Victoria Nursery it was determined in 1930 that its service was "no longer regarded as adequate care" and as a corrective measure the age of children's admission was raised to six months. In 1935, the age of admission was raised further, to eighteen months because "it was realized that institutional care was detrimental to the welfare of children under two years of age."[24] In 1951 only children older than two years were admitted.

The other nurseries imposed similar admission restrictions with analogous justifications. The West End Creche's age of admission was raised to one year old in 1932, and to eighteen months in 1940 "because babies a year old require a larger staff to care for them."[25] This comment indicates a shift in attitude away from that expressed earlier, when caring for a large number of young children was not considered particularly problematic. In 1949-50, the admission age was raised to two-and-a-half because "younger children were not ready to leave close personal attention of the home and were too young to benefit from the group programme of the nursery."[26] In 1950,

East End Day Nursery 1936. Children eating in small groups at child-sized tables.

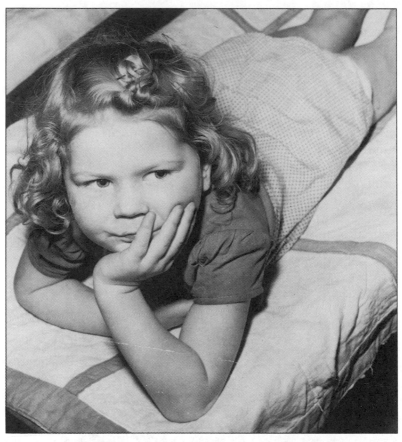

East End Day Nursery (c. 1940s). Children slept on individual cots.

the age of admission to the East End nursery was raised to two years, and in 1954 to three years. At the Winnipeg nursery the age of admission was raised to ten months in 1952, and to two years in 1955. The Ottawa nursery stopped accepting children under two years from 1960 on. In 1963, it further raised the age to three years, explaining that "the child is not ready for the socializing experience of a large group of children until he is 3 years old. It is for the children of 3 and 4 years of age that the Nursery program has most to offer."[27]

By 1935, caregiving at the Montreal Day Nursery was limited to children who were at least one year old. By or during the

1950s, services were further limited to children two years and older. The adoption of the normative temporal discourse at that nursery is illustrated by it's director's explanations for the elimination of care for younger children: "From close observation, we feel that the two year old child, in most cases, is not able to cope with the group setting in which he finds himself, and that all day separation from his mother (8-10 hours) is a very real problem for both of them."[28] The next year it was further explained that "the two year old child does not function as well in a large group. He has not yet come to the age when he can share his toys, and he finds it difficult to share the affection and attention of the teacher with others," and that three year olds "are of an age to benefit from nursery experience and more able to cope with all day separation from their mothers."[29]

As well as raising the ages of admission, day nursery provisions for children older than six years were abolished in the 1940s and 1950s at all except the West End Creche. The nurseries' records provide little insight into the reasoning behind the elimination of care for school age children. One likely reason was the detrimental impact that mixing of age groups was viewed to have on both the younger and older children. Another, and probably more influential reason in Ontario was that after 1946 provincial funding was only made available for the care of preschool children. In order to receive as large a grant as possible and still preserve a lower child-caregiver ratio, the nurseries would have had to make all spaces available to the preschool group.

Another change related to the temporal structuring of children's genetic and personality development, was the like-age grouping of children, as practiced at the Institute's nursery school. The Montreal nursery reported six groupings of children in 1951: one each for the two, three, and four year olds, and two groups of five year olds.[30] At both the Winnipeg and Ottawa nurseries, in the 1950s children were grouped by ages. Along with the like-age grouping of children was a decrease in group sizes. Margaret Twitchell, graduate of the Institute and director of the East End nursery, identified smaller group size as the first aspect of its reorganization, describing this as a change from formerly poor care, to good care. She noted that this change had "cut down the number of children from a large group (50 children getting inadequate care) to a group small enough to be handled properly."[31] The "proper" handling of children referred to the ideas of the normative curriculum. The reorganization of children's groups in terms of age and number was viewed as a positive outcome of the narrowed age range of children provided with care. Discontinuing of infant care at the Victoria Nursery in 1935, for example, "made it possible to divide the other pre-school children into a Junior and a Senior group."[32]

The amount of time children spent in the day nurseries also became a concern. Policies were changed to encourage the provision of service for children who would attend on a regular basis. The nurseries were less accommodating of mothers who required irregular child care services. This was very different from the earlier nursery practice of basing enrolment policies on the *mother's* employment needs. For example, at the West End Creche in 1939, preference was given to children who would attend "for long time training rather than as a temporary convenience."[33] At the Ottawa nursery it was determined, in 1948, that "children who are in regular attendance should have priority. Those who come one day occasionally should be discouraged, as it takes two weeks on average to get a child adjusted."[34]

Although long-term attendance was viewed as essential, spending long hours at a nursery was considered detrimental to children. As discussed previously, in its earlier years the hours of the Montreal nursery had been set for the purpose of regulating mothers' employment. In the 1950s, the concern was with regulating the amount of time children spent with their mothers. Its hours of operation were shortened by opening at 8 a.m. instead of 7 a.m., and closing at 5:30 instead of 6:00 p.m, with the explanation that this "shortens the Nursery day for some of the children who were always left until 6 o'clock. Now, they are taken home earlier, and so have more time to spend with their mothers before going to bed. A very important factor when they have not seen mummy [sic] all day."[35] The West End Creche shortened its day by a half hour by opening at 7:30 instead of 7 a.m. in 1939, as did the East End nursery by opening at 7 a.m. instead of 6:30.

Mothers' responses to these temporal changes of service are not available. However, we can assume that some women would have been unable to coordinate their need to work with the nurseries' policies regarding ages and hours of operation. One mother whose child attended the Winnipeg Day Nursery expressed her exasperation with that agencies' temporal regulations. Although her letter does not refer to a *change* in the nursery's hours of operation, it does illustrate the conflict between nursery hours and her employment situation. It also suggests that the mother perceived nursery personnel to consider her employment problematic for her son's well being.

> Your letter of today has caused me a lot of anxiety…. The point about picking up Stewart after 5:45 p.m. is a sore point. I do not finish work until around 5:15 p.m. any evening and even with luck and Winnipeg Transit on my side I cannot reach the nursery much before 5:45 to 5:55. The evening I was so late was caused by the fact that it was the Jewish New Year on the Friday and I work for a Jewish firm. I had to leave the office around 4:30 p.m. to call on a customer and was delayed by circumstances beyond my control… I realize the staff have a long day but surely a mother who has to make use of the nursery services also has a viewpoint. I can assure you if given the opportunity, there is nothing I would rather do than stay at home with Stewart.
>
> I appreciate the kindness and attention given to the children by all the nursery staff and apologise [sic] if I have been lax in any way in showing this appreciation but also ask that the rules may be slightly less rigid when applied to mothers who, by the very necessity of having to use the nursery, have to conform to many rules.[36]

Mothers using the Montreal Day Nursery apparently had similar conflicts between their hours of work and those of the nursery. While sympathy was expressed for the mothers who were negatively affected by the reduction of nursery hours, it was made clear that those responsible for determining the service no longer took social responsibility for these needs of the mothers:

> We are fully aware that economic and other problems often keep the mother out of the home for part or all of the day…. If

day nursery care is not the answer to this need, and we feel that it is not, then the community must look elsewhere for the solution.[37]

The final statement of this passage highlights the relationship between the transformation of the temporal structuring of care and the shift in the nursery's social role, whereby it no longer functioned to provide a service to mothers.

Transformation of Day Nursery Spatial Structures

Another aspect of the Institute's child care curriculum undertaken by the day nurseries was that of spatial organization. Like the scheduling of time, in the period after 1925, space was reorganized from primarily supporting adult functions, to facilitating children's genetic and personality development. This included the modification of the use of space and the adoption of a maturationist discourse with respect to the meaning of space and materials.

A changed spatial structure was identified as transforming the very meaning of day nursery care. At the East End nursery, Margaret Twitchell reported that spatial reorganization "[brought] about the change from a 'preschool' department to a nursery school."[38] At the Montreal nursery, spatial changes were made in 1948, "to fit in with nursery school requirements. Two rooms were converted to playrooms, shelves and educational toys were furnished."[39] By 1948, space at the East End nursery had been divided into specific areas of play, as was that of the Winnipeg nursery by 1953. A 1959 description illustrates the spatial arrangements at the latter agency:

> In one corner a small bespectacled boy applied himself to an ironing board and another 'tut-tutted' on the telephone — while a green mouse painted by a very small girl energetically emerged in another corner. There was a very busy kitchen in still another corner with a tea party in progress close by.... The fourth corner found a small boy and girl completely engrossed in building toys and games....[40]

In 1972 the same nursery, but in a new building designed for providing caregiving services, was described as follows: "On the lower level there are two spacious bright playrooms for the

East End Day Nursery 1948. The house centre at the nursery
resembled that of the Institute's nursery school.

use of the nursery children ages 2 1/2 to 5 years. There are also washrooms and individual lockers for outdoor clothing. Adjacent to the playrooms are two specially designed observation rooms which are used by the many students who come to observe the children."[41]

In contrast to Maizie Hill's recollections of the earlier caregivers' *laissez-faire* approach to children's play, as recounted in Chapter Two, was the specialized provision of toys and play equipment. At the East End nursery, it was reported that "for the pre-school group a thoroughly modern but by no means radical program is being introduced. Toys in this department, for example, are being culled over with an eye to their psychological value."[42] At the Winnipeg nursery "educational toys and equipment are chosen that a child may develop mentally and socially. Some of the toys are of an individual nature so that he may enjoy solitary play if he wishes. Others, such as building blocks, trains, dolls, etc. become more fun if a group of children play with them together."[43] The identification of a crucial correspondence between developmental management, good child care, and play materials was made at the West End Creche:

> A problem which must be tackled in the near future is that of more adequate budgeting for recreational equipment. One of the important skills of a professional nursery worker is her knowledge of suitable play equipment for pre-school children at different stages of development. *To properly practice her profession and to achieve the results for which she is working*, she must have the funds to replace and add to equipment as needed. It is useless to raise the standard of training of staff members if we then limit them in *the very tools of their profession*.[44]

The belief that good child care required a special arrangement of space and particular types of materials is further revealed by the East End director's description of that nursery's transformation:

> The next move [in changing practices] was to re-arrange the available space and to provide necessary equipment: instead of a dark passage a new cloak-room was provided with box cupboards, each one marked with the child's name and his picture; a room, formerly used for the infants' department, was turned into a sleeping room; a section of the playground was fenced off for the younger children and suitably equipped with sand box, swings, jungle gym, etc.; the dining-room was used as an extra playroom so that the children could be divided into junior and senior groups for play.[45]

Most important was the connection between spatial structure and developmental outcome. Proof of the success of these changes in managing development was in the children themselves. The East End director remarked: "it is only when you have a group of four-year olds who have come up through the nursery school that you can judge the results of the different types of training. We have now reached this point, with very gratifying results."[46]

Transformation of Day Nursery Observation

In Chapter Three, it was pointed out that observation of children was an integral feature of the Institute's nursery curriculum. This was a new activity for caregivers of young children. In the late nineteenth and early twentieth centuries, observation of children in day nursery care was limited to their physical growth and was usually carried out by the doctors and nurses. During its early years, the Montreal nursery kept monthly records of infants' weight, noting that the practice resulted in a "gratifying improvement in infant care."[47] In 1922 it was reported that the nursery's doctor kept "charts to record the condition, weight, feeding, etc of the babies."[48] As well, some nurseries required reports of children's intellectual abilities before admitting them.

With the adoption of the Institute's child care curriculum, observations of development were, to some extent, incorporated into caregiving practices. More children and fewer caregivers at the day nurseries made it unlikely that continuous and intensive record keeping could have been implemented. In a letter to Annie Thexton, of the Winnipeg Day Nursery in 1953, the director of the West End Creche explained how her staff carried out observational procedures:

> Some time ago we established a system of recording the children's progress on a regular basis, adapting an outline published in the Child Welfare League monthly bulletin to our needs.
>
> When our records were started the nursery teachers followed this form very closely until they got the feel of it, and then it was agreed it should be used as a general outline and guide but changed to some extent for individual children. Usually it is still followed fairly closely in the initial record written in considerable detail about two months after the child's admission.... Follow-up reports are added periodically, ... more or less frequently and in greater or less detail as seems indicated by the child's problems and development.
>
> ...
>
> On the whole the teachers have found the record-writing useful and stimulating. It has seemed to make them more aware of each child as an individual and has made the teachers' observation of the children more purposeful, has helped to sift out the really significant things in the behaviour, and led to a better understanding of them and to increased insight.[49]

Although the detailed observation procedures recommended for supervising children's development were not fully implemented, observation came to be acknowledged as a necessary aspect of day nursery caregiving. At the West End Creche, the caregivers' observations of children's "emotional adjustment" were recorded "and used for constant reference."[50] That this was viewed as a characteristic of good caregiving at the nursery was evident in one of its annual reports:

> Satisfactory care for children must include miniature experiences of living; there must be maintained a nice balance between: the things children do together (eating, playing, singing); the things children do for themselves (washing, dressing, putting away toys); the things children do for each other (helping smaller children, waiting on tables). This balance is not the product of a well-planned time-table alone; *it is the result of continuous watching on the part of a staff trained to understand children.*[51]

East End Day Nursery 1954. Children playing with small blocks on table.

Children's regular nursery attendance was thought to provide the opportunity for adequate supervisory observation, enabling caregivers "to recognize early signs of emotional problems, and to try to relieve the situation by referral to the right sources."[52] Children whose troubling behaviour could not be modified within the normal activities of the nursery, would be seen by the nursery's social worker for assessment, with the possibility of referral to a mental hygiene clinic. Along with the transformation of the caregiver's role into that of observer was a reclassification of children's behaviours as problematic or non-problematic according to mental hygiene characteristics. The behaviour of the children was now being evaluated according to psychological criteria of normality. At the Montreal nursery it was remarked that "the number of referrals to psychiatry alone ... show how alert both Miss Ramsay [social worker] and the teaching staff have been."[53]

Resistance to the Transformations

The above specification of changes to the nurseries does not mean that adoption of the normative curriculum occurred smoothly. Dorothy Millichamp has commented that even after hiring an Institute graduate, the organizers of the East End nursery found it difficult to shift to the nursery school program.[54] Lois Evans resigned as President of the Winnipeg nursery's Board of Directors in 1953, to protest the decision to hire trained nursery staff. In a letter to the chair of the Community Chest, Mrs. Evans called the cost of ten staff "sheer extravagance" given that daily attendance was reduced to thirty children a day. She concluded, "If professional staff means extravagance then they should not be employed."[55] Nursery staff were also not always accepting of the new ideas. For example, when the West End Creche's Board of Management decided to change the practices of the agency in 1925 to include a nursery school and parent education classes, the superintendent, Miss Phillips, resigned, apparently because "she could not cooperate in the designed reforms."[56]

In the case of the Ottawa Day Nursery, the normative curriculum was not enacted until after the 1946 passage of the Ontario Day Nurseries Act. The organizers of that nursery appear to have been largely uninterested, and perhaps antagonistic, toward the normative curriculum. This is indicated by their initial refusal to become involved with the Ottawa Nursery School Association. They argued that "the association would like to use the Nursery as a proving ground for systems and accordingly they do not favour, at present, any connection with the association."[57] Even after the passing of the 1946 Act, its organizers apparently had to be cajoled by the provincial inspector of nurseries, Elsie Stapleford, to make changes. At a nursery meeting it was reported that,

> Miss Stapleford emphasized the fact that Provincial regulations are already supposed to be abided by and urged that we reorganize as soon as possible. She stated that there are several trained workers in Toronto, any one of which might suit the nursery.... After some discussion it was decided to carry on at the moment.... It was felt this procedure [present use of staff] was preferable to employing a trained worker immediately, before looking into the matter from every angle and choosing someone with care for a trial period.[58]

The Ottawa nursery organizers apparently perceived the Act as forcing compliance, stating that "with establishment of new legislation *imposed* on Day Nursery by the Provincial Government, certain adjustments *must of necessity* be made."[59]

The reason for the reluctance of the Ottawa agency to follow the pattern of the other Ontario nurseries in transforming their practices early on, is not entirely clear. However, it may have been due to the influence of Mrs. Allen Grace Mather. Mather was one of the founding members of the Ottawa nursery. In 1916, she became its Convenor of Management, directly supervising the work of the matron and other household staff. She remained Convenor of Management until shortly before her death in 1948, and it was not until then that the nursery hired its first trained staff.

The hesitancy of the Ottawa nursery to adopt the ideas and practices set out in the Act might also have had to do with antagonisms between its organizers and Toronto Institute Director, William Blatz. There appears to have been at least two influential child care factions in Ottawa throughout this period. One agreed with Blatz and the other disliked him and/or his ideas.[60] The Ottawa nursery organizers' refusal to involve themselves with the Ottawa Nursery School Association (who's membership consisted of Institute graduates) in the 1940s suggests that the day nursery organizers were members of the anti-Blatz faction.

Despite long standing resistance to the normative model, once the nursery school trained Elma Nelson was hired as director in 1948, the organizers acquiesced. The nursery immediately joined the Ottawa Nursery School Association, with Nelson as its representative.[61] From 1949 the records

East End Day Nursery (date unknown). Children playing with table blocks.

indicate the organizer's agreement with changes to the nursery program, stating for example that "the Board of Management has enthusiastically endorsed and approved Mrs. Nelson's aims and her method of accomplishment."[62]

For most of the nurseries it is likely that staff who did not agree with the normative curriculum were not in positions of authority and therefore would have had little say in matters of policy. Their work with the children might have reflected non-compliance, but any such resistance did not prevent the transformation of day nursery policies, or the directors' and organizers' beliefs that such changes were both beneficial and necessary.

With the 1925 opening of the University of Toronto Institute of Child Study, the policies and practices of the day nurseries began to be transformed in accordance with the normative child care curriculum. The initial impact of Blatz and the Institute was a transformation of the nursery organizers' beliefs and values about children and child care. This meant that they began to hire staff trained in child study or in nursery school methods, which, for most of the nurseries, appears to have been one of the leading factors in the implementation of the Institute's model of child care. By the 1940s the normative curriculum had become the customary form of day nursery care. In Ontario, these practices were legally required by 1946. The fact that the Winnipeg and Montreal nurseries also transformed their practices in accordance with the Institute model, despite the lack of legal requirements in their home provinces until after 1960, demonstrates that laws were not necessary in order for the changes to be made at those nurseries. By 1960 the practices of all the nurseries studied here were completely defined by the normative curriculum.

FOOTNOTES

1 WDN. "Nursery a Godsend" *Winnipeg Free Press*, October, 1963.

2 WDN. "Day Nursery Director Sees Gap In Service" newspaper article, February, 1958.

3 ODN. Annual Report, 1962.

4 MDN. "Montreal Day Nursery 1888-1952."

5 VDN. "Programme Committee Meeting" 1956.

6 MDN. Executive Director's Report, 1953.

7 WDN. "Day Nursery Centre" 1953.

8 EEDN. Welfare Council of Toronto and District, 1941.

9 MDN. Newspaper article, *The Standard* [Montreal], November 24, 1945.

10 MDN. Executive Director's Report, 1960.

11 ODN. Annual Report, 1948-49.

12 WDN. Minutes, September 17, 1953.

13 WEC. Report, 1945.

14 ODN. Annual Report, 1965

15 WDN. "Organization of Mothers' Association Day Nursery" 1953-54.

16 WDN. "Minutes of Early History," June 1, 1976.

17 WDN. "Organization of Mothers' Association Day Nursery" 1953-54.

18 WEC. "Report of the West End Creche" 1933-34.

19 EEDN. "Fresh Air, Food, Sleep, Take Turns at Nursery" newspaper article c. 1930.

20 "Day Nursery Reaches Out to Embrace Whole Family" *The Gazette* [Montreal], May 1, 1950.

21 MDN. Executive Director's Report, 1951.

22 EEDN. Annual Report, 1941.

23 See Riley, D. 1983. *War in the Nursery: Theories of the Child and Mother.* London: Virago Press.

24 VDN. "Programme Committee Meeting" 1956.

25 WEC. Annual Report, 1939.

26 WEC. "Highlights, 1909-1959."

27 ODN. Annual Report, 1963.

28 MDN. Executive Director's Report, 1955.

29 MDN. Executive Director's Report, 1955.

30 MDN. Annual Report, 1951.

31 EEDN. Welfare Council of Toronto and District, 1941.

32 VDN. "Programme Committee Meeting" 1956.

33 WEC. Annual Report, 1939.

34 ODN. Minutes, January 13, 1948.

35 MDN. Executive Director's Report, 1956.

36 WDN. Letter from parent to Gretta Brown, October, 1962.

37 MDN. Executive Director's Report, 1956.

38 EEDN. Welfare Council of Toronto and District, 1941.

39 MDN. "The Montreal Day Nursery 1888-1952."

40 WDN. "Five-Year-Olds Perform For Day Nursery" newspaper article, 1959.

41 WDN. "Day Nursery Opens New Unit" newspaper article, March 23, 1972.

42 EEDN. Annual Report, 1934-35.

43 WDN. Monthly Report, April 23, 1964.

44 WEC. Report, 1945. Emphasis added.

45 EEDN. Welfare Council of Toronto and District, 1941.

46 EEDN. Welfare Council of Toronto and District, 1941.

47 MDN. "Montreal Day Nursery 1888-1952."

48 MDN. Annual Meeting, 1922.

49 WDN. Letter from M. Lovatt, August 20, 1953.

50 WEC. Report, 1933-34.

51 WEC. Annual Report, 1939. Emphasis added.

52 MDN. Executive Director's Report, 1956.

53 MDN. Executive Director's Report, 1956.

54 Millichamp, 1977. Interview.

55 WDN. Letter from Lois Evans to Mr. J.M. Sinclair, December 8, 1953.

56 WEC. "History of the West End Creche" 1974.

57 ODN. Minutes, June 10, 1947.

58 ODN. Minutes, September 17, 1947.

59 ODN. Annual Report, 1947-48. Emphasis added.

60 Ontario, Department of Education manuscript collection, RG2 S1 Box 5, 1950-52. Ontario Provincial Archives, Canada.

61 ODN. Minutes, May 11, 1948.

62 ODN. Annual Report, 1948-49.

Chapter Six

The Rediscovery of the Child

In an effort to break the poverty cycle thus engendered the federal government provided unprecedented funds for the education of children from disadvantaged homes — especially preschool-age children. Thus the value of early education quickly became accepted and the young child was "rediscovered" by educators, the public, and the parents.[1]

The 1960s marks another important moment in the history of ideas about child care. With proclamations made about the 'rediscovery' of the early childhood years, this period of life became symbolic of a frontier of human potential yet to be fully exploited for its riches. With an evangelical intensity not seen since the early twentieth century, the science of child study promised, by revealing the heretofore hidden potential of the child, to lead society to a prosperous future.

Unlike the period from 1925 to the 1960s, when the Toronto Institute was so very influential over Canadian nursery practices, after 1960 it was the dissemination of ideas through U.S. and other Canadian research centres and training institutions that gained authority. One of the reasons for this appears to have been because of the reduction in the Toronto Institute's research role. Understanding the Institute's decline as the centre of Canadian child study research and day nursery training provides the context for changes undertaken to day nursery policies and practices after 1960.

In 1960, William Blatz resigned from the Institute, and because of ill health, virtually disappeared from academic and public life. He died in 1964. With his departure, the Institute lost its strongest voice, no doubt increasing its vulnerability during a time of debate and contestation within the child study research community. In 1958, the Institute underwent a review by the University of Toronto administration which resulted in a negative assessment of the research conducted by the Institute. The observational study of children's behaviours (the dominant form of study carried out at the Institute) was criticized as being unable to produce the hard, cold, 'scientific' facts that could be derived from experimental studies. An outcome of the report was the withdrawal, in 1965, of University financial support for the Institute's observational research, with further funding made contingent upon Institute research becoming experimental. The justification was essentially, that the old method was outdated. The University's President explained it this way, "The Institute's approach, and its way of organizing research, are said to be no longer useful, since long-term developmental research with a highly selected child population has been replaced by other approaches that have been found more fruitful."[2]

The new funding imperative virtually eliminated the child study research carried out at the Institute, as well as its publicization activities. While some research continued, teaching became its primary fuction. Long time faculty Dorothy Millichamp and Mary Northway were unable to reconcile themselves to the 'new' Institute. By the end of the 1960s they had both resigned their positions and had established the Brora Centre, a non-profit research foundation. Structured to operate for a five year period, it financially supported "research in human growth and development and produc[ed] both scholarly and popular publications" as well as other services formerly provided by the Institute, such as psychological guidance for children and consultations with agencies involved with programs for children.[3] A foundation with no formal university affiliation, the Brora Centre did not attain the status and authority held by the Toronto Institute under the leadership of William Blatz.

Although the Institute's primary mission became one of teacher-training from the 1960s on, this did not mean a greater role in the training of day nursery caregivers. In 1971, the Institute was assimilated into the Ontario College of Education (Faculty of Education at University of Toronto) where its teaching focus was on the training of kindergarten and elementary school teachers. From then on, the Institute no longer offered non-degree courses for caregivers or the Master's degree in Psychology.

Through the initiation of Institute alumni and faculty, nursery training programs were established at other post-secondary institutions. The first to be organized was the 1959 two year training course for nursery school teachers at Toronto's Ryerson Polytechnic Institute. In 1968, the Nursery Education Association of Ontario, made up of Institute alumni, successfully initiated a number of eighteen week courses offered through the extension departments of the Universities of Toronto, McMaster, Guelph and Queen's.[4] Post-secondary day nursery training courses continued to be developed throughout the late 1970s and after in all Canadian provinces. Not all of these were initiated by Institute graduates, and not all adopted the philosophy of care that had been promoted by the Institute. The number of training programs increased, but since the Institute no longer supplied Masters' graduates who might teach in them, it became necessary for faculty to be hired from outside of Canada, primarily from the United States. This spurred the importation of ideas about the nature of the child and alternate caregiving practices, and further multiplied the sources of ideas available to day nursery caregivers. The theoretical basis of those ideas is described in this chapter.

The New Nature of the Child

In the 1950s child study researchers began to focus increased attention on the early learning abilities of infants and young children. The theories of Jerome Bruner, Jean Piaget, J. McVicker Hunt, and Benjamin Bloom about the nature of the child, became popular in public, professional and academic discourse.

Bruner's *The Process of Education* was one of the landmark publications of the new decade. It was an outcome of a conference in the United States, organized in response to the Soviet

Sputnik success, that discussed "how education in science might be improved in our [U.S.] primary and secondary schools."[5] Although he did not focus on preschool education, Bruner sparked an interest in children's abilities to learn any school subject, at any age, if the apporpriate teaching methods were used. Bruner's hypothesis "that any subject can be taught effectively in some intellectually honest form to any child at any stage of development,"[6] was antithetical to the maturationist argument that learning, especially of formal school subjects, could only take place at certain points along the continuum of development. According to maturationist theory, it was both a waste of developmental energy and also detrimental to development, for children to be exposed to an environment that did not correspond to their current developmental levels. The normative curriculum of the Toronto Institute's nursery school, was designed to provide just such a correspondence. Bruner's hypothesis did not displace the maturationist theory within the field of child study. However, it did result in the reconceptualization of schedules of development from being genetically determined with the environment providing the opportunities for the expression of the development, to being open to manipulation with the environment having a primary influence on the nature of development.

The most influential theory from the 1960s has been Jean Piaget's developmentalist theory (also referred to as interactionist theory). Textbooks for child study and early education students have become replete with what amounts to an idolatry of his theoretical perspective, along with descriptions of ways to apply these theories through what are termed developmentalist activities. The popularization of Piaget's theories, especially about children's cognitive abilities, stimulated a change in dominant ideas about the nature of child development.[7] The theoretical proposition most focused on in North America was that development arises out of children's continuous interactions with their environment. This was not a simple behaviorist stimulus-response notion. Rather, environmental interaction was perceived to produce structural transformations in the thinking processes of children.

Piaget formulated the concepts of *assimilation* (the active process of seeking to incorporate new experience into one's ways of thinking) and *accommodation* (alterations of an individual's existing cognitive structures) as explanations for how individuals actively construct their knowledge of the world. According to Piaget the child actively seeks out information about the world. His or her thinking processes are an outcome of the continuous interplay between old and new experiences. It is the child's interaction with the environment that enables cognitive development to occur in what Piaget considered to be an invariant and universal sequence of stages, or periods, of particular kinds of mental structures. As the individual proceeds through the stages, there occurs a qualitative structural change in how he/she thinks. In other words, the type of thinking that the individual can carry out is forever transformed. Piaget identified four major periods of cognitive development and their estimated chronology, with each successive period considered to be a more fully developed process of thinking: sensorimotor (birth to two years), preoperational (two to seven years), concrete operational (seven to eleven years), and formal operational (eleven to fifteen years).

Piaget's reference to ages when certain periods of development occurred differed from the maturationist concept of ages-and-stages, in that Piaget did not base *explanations* for developmental change on the increasing age of the child, but used age as a marker indicating the period of life when children typically had similar types of experiences. McVicker Hunt's comparison of the two viewpoints clarifies the difference:

> A careful normative description of the behavior characteristic of each age constitutes for Gesell an explanation as well as a description. For Piaget ... the relationship between a behavioral landmark and the age it appears is simply a convenient device; the explanation of development comes rather in the child-environment interaction.[8]

Like the impact of Hall and Gesell at the end of the nineteenth and beginning of the twentieth centuries, the popularization of Piaget in North America provided a unique way of understanding development. We do not just know *more* about the child, we know the child *differently*.

Piaget had been publishing his developmentalist theory since the 1930s, and his ideas were known by William Blatz and other child study researchers prior to their broader publication and popularization in the 1960s. In fact, child-adult interactions were planned within the Institute's nursery school curriculum as a means of exploring Piaget's theories of language and thinking. However, the fact that they did not become part of the mainstream of child study, or of the child care curriculum until the 1960s demonstrates the dominant position held by the maturationist theory. One reason for the shift in interest toward Piaget's theories, was that they provided a more conducive approach for applying Bruner's hypothesis of manipulating development. In this regard, the child care curriculum of the Institute's nursery school began to appear as outdated, based as it was on the belief that the environment needed to be matched to the 'normally' developing child's age, rather than designed to provide experiences that would increase developmental abilities.

During the same period that the ideas of Bruner and Piaget were popularized, there arose in the United States a widespread concern about the continued existence of poverty in a society that had made tremendous economic progress during the post-war years. It was noted that children from economically disadvantaged families failed in school more often than other children. The explanation for this failure, known as the theory of cultural deprivation, was that economically disadvantaged children lacked experiences with materials and interactions that provided the cognitive and personality development necessary for school success. It was hypothesized that this lack of cultural preparation continued the cycle of poverty: school failure led to underemployment or unemployment, which led to poverty, which reproduced the conditions productive of the next generation of 'culturally deprived' children.

The concept of cultural deprivation has come under heavy criticism by both scholars and social activists. The main concern is the premise that the root cause of poverty lies within individual personality deficiencies of the poor rather than with the North American class structure.[9] These criticisms have not, however, prevented the theory from becoming an established part of child development and child care ideas.

J. McVicker Hunt was very influential in creating the shift in cultural ideas around child development, incorporating the culture of poverty thesis into child care. From his position as Professor of Psychology at the University of Illinois, and Director of the Coordinating Center for the National Laboratory for Early Childhood Education, he authored numerous publications articulating Piaget's theories and advocating systems of education for 'culturally deprived' children based on those theories. Using Piaget's concepts of assimilation and accommodation, McVicker Hunt argued that early intelligence was malleable. He concluded that the higher the level of environmental variation experienced by a child, the greater the potential for being interested in learning and for developing the ability to deal with a complex environment.[10]

Basing his ideas on Piaget's theories of stages of cognitive development, McVicker Hunt proposed that children proceed through critical periods in their intellectual development. He classified the preschool years (the period Piaget identified as that of preoperational thinking) as the time when children most needed to be exposed to a variety of materials and interactional experiences if they were to proceed to the next stage of concrete operational thought. The preschool years were therefore crucial because a lack of adequate environmental interaction was viewed to have more permanent effects then than later on. The material and social environment was important for both the developmentalist and maturationist approaches, but in the former the focus was on its ability to stimulate intellectual and cognitive development, rather than to support social and emotional development. According to McVicker Hunt, missed opportunities during the preschool years would lead to a failure to develop flexible schemata which would result in permanent cognitive limitations.

McVicker Hunt connected this argument with conjectures about the environmental experiences of children from low-income families. He drew the conclusion that low-income parents could not provide an environment conducive for optimum cognitive stimulation of children. The greatest concern identified by McVicker Hunt was for the child of three to four years, the time when, he argued, they were most sensitive to learning from interaction because they were expressing verbal communication, independence, question asking, and physical exploration. The assumed problem was that low-income parents were not able to respond to the child's initiations in a way that would further development. Unlike other cultural deprivation theorists, McVicker Hunt did not blame the parents, but thought that the stresses and strains and lack of material opportunities of low-income life produced this result. Although he acknowledged the social conditions of poverty, he maintained that the solution was to supplement chinldren's early experiences with compensatory preschool programs. He concluded, "If nursery schools or day-care centers were arranged for culturally deprived children from 4 — or preferably from age 3 — until time for school at 5 or 6 some of the worst effects of their training might be substantially reduced."[11]

Except for favouring Montessori programs, McVicker Hunt did not outline an early education program of intervention. He did argue for the importance of organizing children's experiences so there would be a match between their interests and experiences with new opportunities, as this would enable assimilation and allow for accommodation. Again, this concept of the "match" needs to be distinguished from its use in the maturationist approach, where experiences were to correspond with the chronological age of the children in order to ensure that genetic potential could be realized. In the developmentalist approach, the match was to be with ability (not age) for the purpose of stimulating development. McVicker Hunt did view the exposure of 'culturally deprived' children to middle class materials, behaviours and grammar as being the most important features for overcoming the developmental limitations imposed by their social and economic class experiences.

In 1964, the child study focus on cognitive development and cultural deprivation was given further emphasis with the claims about intelligence made by Benjamin Bloom.[12] Using longitudinal research to provide a statistical ratio of intellectual development, Bloom claimed "culturally deprived" children had intelligence quotients (I.Q.s) that were twenty points lower than those whom he labeled "culturally abundant" children. In looking at different age ranges for these two groups, he reported that for children up to four years of age, the I.Q. difference between the two groups was ten points; for the ages four to seven, the I.Q. difference was six points; for the ages eight to seventeen, the difference was four points.[13] The fact that children with higher I.Q. scores were from economically privileged groups, and that their greater proficiency on I.Q. tests was sustained throughout childhood and adolescence, was to social structural theorists, evidence that the education system was serving the interests of the economically privileged.[14] In contrast, Bloom argued that the difference was proof that intellectual ability was permanently formed during the first four years of life. Even more startling was his claim that based on the calculated point difference over the years of childhood — fifty percent of intellectual development was completed by the age of four years! Culturally abundant preschoolers would be more intelligent because they were likely to have 'filled out' their intellectual capacity. Thus according to Bloom's theory, after the age of four, only fifty percent of potential intellectual ability remained. Even if not all of the previous fifty percent had been utilized (assuming that this could actually be measured), anything remaining lost its potential. For example, if only twenty-five percent of capacity was 'filled' by age four, the child was not left with a seventy-five percent potential for development, but only fifty percent. Any cultural advantages accrued after the age of four, and especially after the age of eight, were too late to make a difference to the individual's intellectual abilities.

For the most part, prior to the 1960s, intellectual ability was viewed as genetically predetermined.[15] Bloom's conception of intelligence significantly differed from this, in that he emphasized environment over heredity in affecting its development. Instead of intellectual stimulation during the preschool years being considered a waste of developmental energy, the absence of certain types of experiences were judged to result in creating a wasteland of development. Bloom's theory of intellectual capacity, as popularly expounded during the 1960s and 1970s, viewed childhood as a window of opportunity that was half closed by the age of four, and offered only a few openings beyond the age of eight. Whereas Bruner created enthusiasm about the possibilities for learning in childhood, Bloom sounded a dire warning about what would happen if these early years were not properly utilized.

Early Childhood Education

From the rediscovery of the child as described above, there arose the discourse of early childhood education. From the 1960s, no longer were programs for children under five years to focus primarily on emotional and social development. Now the infant and young child was viewed as being able to gain intellectually and cognitively from specific types of adult directed activities. The transformation in beliefs about the nature of the child, and the expectations of success for early childhood education can be found in the 1966 resolution of the [U.S.] National Education Association:

> Education in this two-year-period [four and five year olds] can affect the character of the child and all his future life more deeply than his education at any later period....
>
> With universal early childhood education almost every child would have a higher starting point in knowledge and developed ability.[16]

With this shift in ideas about the nature of the child, the previously accepted emphasis on mental hygiene came under attack. Martin Deutsch, Professor of Psychiatry at New York Medical College, viewed the past belief as having actually been detrimental to children and society:

> The overgeneralized influence on some sections of early childhood education of the emphasis in the child guidance movement upon protecting the child from stress, creating a supportive environment, and resolving emotional conflicts has done more to misdirect and retard the fields of child care, guidance and development than any other single influence. The effect has especially operated to make these fields ineffective in responding to the problems of integrating and educating the non-white urban child.[17]

Deutsch continued his argument by emphasizing William Fowler's 1962 criticisms that the potential for maximizing preschool children's cognitive development had, in the past, not been taken advantage of by child study experts:

In harking constantly to the dangers of premature cognitive training, the image of the "happy," socially adjusted child has tended to expunge the image of the thoughtful and intellectually educated child. Inevitably, in this atmosphere, research (and education) in cognition has lagged badly, especially since the 1930s, not only for the early years of childhood but for all ages.[18]

Just as the maturationist and mental hygiene orientation initiated new ways of understanding children at the beginning of the twentieth century, these excerpts illustrate that the 'truth' about childhood was undergoing a revision from the 1960s.

In the United States the ideas about cognitive and intellectual development and cultural deprivation were brought together with the federal government's War on Poverty. In 1964, as part of this campaign, a panel of child development experts were brought together to discuss the effects of cultural deprivation and the potential of early intervention. The outcome was the adoption, in 1965, of the national program known as Project Head Start.[19] It was designed as a comprehensive program that included health and social services. The discussion here focuses on its educational component.

Head Start early education was intended to be a solution to the assumed role of cultural deprivation in the cycle of poverty by providing low-income children with experiences that would develop the intellectual, cognitive, and personality attributes viewed as enabling typical middle class children to attain academic success. It was argued that this 'compensatory' education would lead to school success, which would lead to better jobs, and better income. By exposing low-income children to a set of experiences that their 'culturally deprived' families could not provide, Head Start programs were designated as agents of individual and social change.

The educational program of Head Start was never specifically defined by its originators. Their broad intentions were that the curriculum should improve the children's mental processes and skills, especially in conceptual and verbal areas. To that end, the Head Start planning committee set out seven objectives that were to guide all Head Start programs:

1. Improving the child's physical health and physical abilities.

2. Helping the emotional and social development of the child by encouraging self-confidence, spontaneity, curiosity and self-discipline.

3. Improving the child's mental processes and skills with particular attention to conceptual and verbal skills.

4. Establishing patterns and expectations of success for the child which will create a climate of confidence for his future learning efforts.

5. Increasing the child's capacity to relate positively to family members and others, while at the same time strengthening the family's ability to relate positively to the child and his problems.

6. Developing in the child and his family a responsible attitude toward society, and fostering constructive opportunities for society to work together with the poor in solving their problems.

7. Increasing the sense of dignity and self-worth within the child and his family.[20]

Within these guidelines, a variety of intervention approaches were undertaken, with the overriding philosophy being that economically privileged and disadvantaged children had differences in quantity and quality of experiences, with the disadvantaged child's experiences being considered deficient in both regards.[21] Intervention programs were designed to provide these children with experiences similar to those of middle class children, to emphasize academic preparation, and to transform the nature of the child.

The direction of U.S. child study research and resultant education policies was followed in Canada. Mary J. Wright, Professor of Psychology at the University of Western Ontario (and an Institute graduate) completed an influential study into the assumptions of Head Start — that young children from low-income families receive inadequate cognitive stimulation, and that these could be compensated through educational intervention. The research involved the implementation and assessment of a cognitive-developmental education program carried out at the Laboratory Preschool at Wright's university. She concluded from the research that while compensatory education during the preschool years was unlikely to eradicate poverty, it did provide substantial and lasting benefits for the children. Her voice was added to those of American researchers who advocated the cost-benefits of cognitively oriented early education programs for low-income children.[22] This study provided a Canadian version of Head Start research, formally aligning Canadian child study with the U.S. investigations.

William Fowler, Professor in the Department of Applied Psychology at the Ontario Institute for the Studies in Education, carried out a five year investigation on the impact of day care on infants and preschoolers.[23] He concluded that a program with "moderate levels of interpersonal care and cognitive stimulation as well as adequate caregiver-child ratios" was not harmful and possibly better for children than home care.[24] This was very different from the child study experts' perceptions of care during the 1950s, that saw home care for infants as better than day nursery care. This was important in the history of child study, because his was the first published Canadian research that attempted to measure and compare the effects of group care and home care of infants and preschoolers. The publication of these findings assisted in the revision of day nursery polices that had eliminated the provision of care for children under the age of three.

Fowler's companion publication to this research was a guidebook for day nursery caregivers.[25] It set out his recommendations for a "high quality" early childhood program that combined the newer focus on early learning, with its attention to "language, concept, and sensory motor skills in order to foster cognitive development," along with Blatz's earlier emphasis on "the development of autonomy in self care."[26] He differed from Blatz, however, in his promotion of the development of autonomy in self care during infancy. This publication appears to have been the first Canadian guide to day nursery practice that was not authored by a member of the University of Toronto Institute of Child Study. In this regard, and in its making available methods of care that utilized Piagetian concepts, Fowler's book mapped a new route for Canadian caregivers to follow.[27]

In this chapter, I have pointed out the changing emphasis of child study research from the 1960s onwards. Ideas about the nature of the child shifted from the earlier focus on development resulting from biological maturation, to the concept of development as arising out of interactions with the environment. The dominant concern about children's development also changed, from the pre-1960s emphasis on supporting social and emotional development for the purpose of society's well-being, to a primary concern for children's intellectual development during the infant and the preschool years, and its relationship to individual economic success. This period of time also saw the adoption of new ways of describing and thinking about the care of young children. Children from low-income families were no longer viewed as being morally endangered, but as being at risk for cognitive and intellectual deficiencies. What had formerly been day nursery care had, by the 1970s, become early childhood education.

FOOTNOTES

1 Leeper, S.H., Dales, R.J., Skipper, D.S. & Witherspoon, R.L. 1968. *Good Schools for Young Children: A Guide for Working with Three-, Four-, and Five-Year-Old Children.* 2nd Edition. NY: MacMillan, p. 3–4.

2 BLATZ. *University of Toronto Bulletin,* December 3, 1968.

3 BLATZ. "Introducing the Brora Centre" nd.

4 *Child Study* (Toronto), 1968, *30*(1):15.

5 Bruner, Jerome, S. 1960. *The Process of Education.* NY: Vintage Books, p. vii.

6 Bruner, 1960. p. 33.

7 For example, Piaget, Jean. 1936/1952. *The Origins of Intelligence in Children.* NY: International Universities Press.

8 Hunt, J. McVicker. 1964/1969. "The Implications of Changing Ideas on How Children Develop Intellectually." In M. S. Aueleta (Ed.), *Foundations of Early Childhood Education: Readings.* NY: Random House, p. 263.

9 Leacock, E. 1967. "Distortions of Working-Class Reality in American Social Science." *Science & Society 31*(1):1–21; 1971. *The Culture of Poverty: A Critique.* NY: Simon & Schuster; 1976. "The Concept of Culture and Its Significance for School Counselors." In J. I. Roberts and S. K. Akinsanya (Eds.), *Schooling in the Cultural Context: Anthropological Studies in Education.* NY: David McKay, pp. 418–426.

10 Hunt, J. McVicker. 1961. *Intelligence and Experience.* NY: Ronald Press.

11 Hunt, 1964/1969, p. 71.

12 Bloom, B. S. 1964. *Stability and Change in Human Characteristics.* NY: Wiley

13 Hechinger, F. M. 1966. "Passport to Equality." In F. M. Hechinger (Ed.), *Pre-school Education Today: New Approaches to Teaching Three-, Four-, and Five-Year-Olds.* NY: Doubleday, p. 4.

14 See for example Apple, M. W. 1982/1985. *Education and Power.* Boston: ARK Paperbacks.

15 This was not the perception of William Blatz, who argued that intelligence was like other ablities, in that it was affected by environmental influences. However, his perspective was not the dominant one in North America. As well, because the focus of the Institute's nursery school curriculum was on children's social and emotional development, his views on intelligence were not widely known.

16 Educational Policies Commission. 1968. "Universal Opportunity for Early Childhood Education." In J. L. Frost (Ed.), *Early Childhood Education Rediscovered: Readings.* Toronto: Holt, Rinehart & Winston, pp. 5–11.

17 Deutsch, M. 1966. "Facilitating Development in the Preschool-Child: Social and Psychological Perspectives." In F. M. Hechinger (Ed.), *Preschool Education Today.* NY: Doubleday, pp. 92–93.

18 Fowler, W. quoted in Deutsch 1966, p. 93.

19 Osborn, K. 1968. "Project Head Start — An Assessment." In Frost (Ed.), pp. 281–286.; Evans, Ellis D. 1975. *Contemporary Influences in Early Childhood Education,* 2nd Edition. Tor: Holt, Rinehart & Winston.

20 Evans, 1975, p. 62.

21 Luis, L. M. 1984. "Social Policies Toward Children of Diverse Ethnic, Racial, and Language Groups in the United States." In H. W. Stevenson & A. E. Siegel (Eds.), *Child Development Research and Social Policy,* vol. 1. Chicago: University of Chicago Press, pp. 1–109.

22 Wright, M. J. 1983. *A Canadian Approach, Compensatory Education in the Preschool: The University of Western Ontario Preschool Project.* Ypsilanti, Michigan: High/Scope Press.

23 Fowler, W. 1978a. *Day Care and Its Effects on Early Development.* Toronto: Ontario Institute for the Study of Education.

24 Fowler, 1978a, p. 60.

25 Fowler, W. 1978b. *Guides to Early Day Care and Teaching.* Toronto: Ontario Institute for the Study of Education.

26 Fowler, 1978b, p. 1–2.

27 See also Fowler, W. 1980. *Infant and Child Care: A Guide to Education in Group Settings.* Toronto: Allyn & Bacon.

Chapter Seven

Day Nursery Care at the End of the Twentieth Century

> Systematization comes upon the scene during an age which feels itself in command of a ready-made and hand-down body of authoritative thought. A creative age must first have passed; then and only then does the business of formalistic systematizing begin — an undertaking typical of heirs and epigones who feel themselves in possession of someone else's, now voiceless word.[1]

By the 1960s, the process of constructing the model of day nursery child care practiced at the end of the twentieth century in Canada was completed. From then on, systemization of the model described in previous chapters was enacted. While changes were made to the content of the child care curriculum, there were no major transformations in its form. Changes did occur in the political-economy of day nursery care, and in social values about the provision of care. One of the results was an extension and diversification of nursery services. For example, by 1993 the programs offered through the Ottawa nursery included the provision of licensed group and family day care, playgroups, a resource centre for parents and caregivers, a country bound summer camp, a child care information service, a support service for the integration of special needs children into group care, short term child care, and the Child Care Professional Reference Centre.[2] While this range of services and other changes to nurseries that are described below appear on the surface to be a return to their pre-1920s social role, there was a difference of philosophical intent. In the pre-1920s period, the nurseries provided a myriad of services with the primary objective of meeting the employment needs of mothers. From 1960 on, the return of nursery services to caring for infants and school age children, and the new provision of care for the middle class child, was done within the philosophical framework of the post-1920s — of supporting the development of the child.

Day Nursery Child Care

The developmentalist theories and the emphasis on intellectual formation described in the previous chapter fueled changes in the child care services provided by Canadian day nurseries. Since the 1960s, Canadian day nurseries began to integrate the discourses of early learning, developmentalist theory, and cultural deprivation into their caregiving policies and practices. However, this did not challenge the overall purpose of supervising and managing development. Instead, the new features were integrated into the already established form regarding the organization of time, space, observations and interactions.

At the Ottawa Day Nursery, the early education objective was manifested in 1965, with the hiring of Frigga von Luczenbacher as Educational Supervisor. This position was approved by the Ottawa Community Chest. That the Chest paid the salary for this position indicated that it was viewed as a legitimate aspect of the day nursery's work. The endorsement of the prevailing ideas about the nature of childhood is further revealed in the statements made by the nursery organizers through the 1960s. In 1966 the formal educational aspect of the program was emphasized by the President of the nursery's Board of Directors:

> The concept of the importance of pre-school training grew to
> the point where we now have a particularly fine Nursery

School programme and our children start Kindergarten in nearby Public and Separate Schools prepared in attitude and background for their wider school experience often far better than their contemporaries.[3]

In 1968, the nursery was described as "a place where small children pass their days in happy pursuits … not simply aimless fun and games but rather very carefully directed activities in the form of pre-school education and training for the future life of these children in their community."[4] The cultural deprivation focus was incorporated through day nursery provisions of Head Start programs modelled after those in the United States. Charlotte Birchard, Director of the Ottawa nursery, explained why her agency opened such a program in 1965: "We are exploring our own way of meeting the needs of some of the children in our community who are today being described by our new found terms of 'disadvantaged' and 'culturally deprived.'[5] In 1970 the Head Start program was described as a "2 hour daily structured, learning situation at a pre-school level. The major focus has been to assist these children in acquiring a desire to learn, some basic skills appropriate to their age level and greater facility in socialization prior to entering the regular school system."[6]

Working Women and Day Nursery Care

The early day nurseries' limitation of their services to poor parents was an outcome of both financial exigency and social values. The nurseries could not afford to pay for the staff, or materials necessary to care for all the children whose parents desired to use the service. Therefore, the admission of children had to be limited. The decision as to who would receive the service was based on the belief that unless absolutely essential, mothers should not work while their children were young. The definition of essential was usually limited to economics. All the day nurseries studied here had policies that required two parent families to demonstrate that both needed to work in order to provide their families with the basic necessities of food, shelter and clothing. The only exceptions made for middle class children were for those referred to a day nursery because of medical or psychological conditions that were thought rectifiable by the program. Despite the prevailing social values of the time that inhibited middle class mothers from seeking paid employment, there were always some who went against the norm and requested the services of the nurseries so that they could work. They were inevitably turned down. The social values about working mothers began to change in the 1960s, and increasing numbers of middle class women applied for nursery caregiving services. Organizers of the day nurseries were faced with the dilemma of dealing with their own conflicting beliefs and values about women and motherhood, and the reality of the financial structure of their agencies. In these charitable organizations receipt of monies depended upon maintaining policies of only admitting children of financially 'needy' families. The conflicting sentiments of the 1960s were expressed in a Winnipeg Day Nursery document:

> This question of, "Why are you working" is asked of every person coming to our Agency to apply for care. The answers we get are numerous and varied. To buy a home; shortage of professional workers and community needs me; bored. Is it our responsibility to care for children of mothers who are working for these reasons? I think we can accept the fact that at least some of these reasons are legitimate, and I am convinced that there should be more private Nurseries in this city. However, it is not the policy of DNC [Day Nursery Centre] to give service to this type of person.[7]

As beliefs about the role of women were challenged and the economic social structure began to change, so did nursery admission policies. The women's movement was gaining momentum, and part of its focus was on the right of all women to engage in paid employment. Women with young children were effectively transforming beliefs and values about their social roles by entering the work force in greater numbers than ever before. The 1970 Royal Commission on the Status of Women recognized child care as a necessity in order for women to utilize their right to work. These factors brought political pressure to bear on all levels of government to provide the legislation and funding necessary for more day nursery spaces so that all mothers could have access to child care services and thus be enabled to participate in employment.[8]

Pressure for expanded day nursery services resulted in the resumption of day nursery care for school age children. In Winnipeg, by 1962, lunch and after school programs for children in grades one, two and three were operating out of Crescent Fort Rouge United Church, Westminster United Church, and Home Street United Church. The Winnipeg nursery "did intake [selection of children] for these programs and ... [gave] continuing support in a consultant capacity."[9] In 1972, the Winnipeg nursery was also overseeing such programs out of Windsor Park Church and out of its own Flora Avenue location. In 1983, there were 14,987 licensed day nursery spaces throughout Canada, for children aged six years and over.[10]

The Ottawa Day Nursery responded to the changing social values by altering their policy for selecting children that would receive care. In 1964 this was carried out for the purpose of "helping" families who did not need the service because of their financial situation.

> It was decided that, for the time being, the $5000 income ceiling on admissions be lifted, so that children, other than those of mothers working through necessity, might come into care when need of nursery care of the children was indicated. It was felt that some families on the verge of trouble might be helped before some serious disruption and that the intake policy be considered in terms of human values, as well as financial.[11]

While still limiting care to children whose families were experiencing problems, the vague wording of the new policy indicates that it became theoretically possible for mothers to utilize the day nursery based on the argument that they were working in order to maintain family harmony. By 1965, ideas at this nursery had changed with the times: "every child of every working mother has a right to such care."[12] Note that in line with the day nursery's social role of developmental supervision and management, in this instance the focus of 'rights' was on the child.

More broadly, the emerging social values about the right of women to work were combined with new research findings that contradicted previous arguments about the negative effects of day care on infants. The speaker at the Ottawa nursery's 1965 annual meeting addressed this issue, citing the arguments of experts, notably Bowlby's revision of his initial claims that mother-child separation was necessarily traumatic. If group care was not necessarily harmful, there was less justification for limiting day nursery services to children whose mothers needed to work for financial reasons. An outcome was that day nurseries once again began to care for children younger than two or three years of age. At first, such care was provided separate from the centre-based day nursery services. In 1959, the organizers of the Victoria nursery were attempting to restructure their service from that of primarily a day nursery to including a family day care agency. A psychiatric consultant was appointed to the staff in order to participate in the planning for such a venture. The nursery submitted a proposal, in 1960-61, to the Ontario provincial government to have the family day care service funded, but it was turned down. In 1963-64 the proposal was again submitted, and this time approved, marking the new beginning of this phase of the program which provided caregiving services for children under two years of age.

At the Ottawa nursery, a family day care service was begun as a demonstration project in 1969, supported with government funds. It was identified as being "the only Family Day Care Demonstration Project in the Province and served as a model for the development of new services in Ontario."[13] By 1978, family day care had become an established part of the Ottawa nursery, serving 200 children between the ages of three months and ten years.

By the 1980s, care for infants was also available in some centre-based day nursery programs. Changes to provincial day nursery regulations allowed for the funding and provision of these services. By 1983 in Canada, there were 8,322 licensed day nursery spaces for children under two years of age.[14]

While day nursery services were once again extended to include infants, this was carried out within the framework of the normative curriculum. In other words, while the child care curriculum for infants would differ from that of preschoolers in terms of content, it would be similar in having as its primary purpose the supervision and management of development.

The adoption of the normative child care curriculum resulted in many positive benefits for children in day nursery care. It meant that the needs of children were taken into account to a greater extent than previously; it emphasized the value of small groups in child care; it expanded the focus from children's physical and moral health to their emotional and social needs; it gave importance to the provision of specialized materials and equipment. While overall these changes have made the Canadian day nurseries better places for children, there have also been negative consequences. Recognition of these consequences makes it possible to question whether the normative perspective is the best framework for child care.

Consequences of the Normative Perspective

By the 1980s, normative caregiving practices were being referred to as the developmentally appropriate curriculum. Caregiving practices that were not based on normative beliefs were considered inappropriate. Caregivers were informed of the content of developmentally appropriate practice through guidelines published by the major professional authority in early childhood education, the U.S. based National Association for the Education of Young Children, and by the Canadian Child Care Federation.[15]

The application of normative theories in developmentally appropriate practices is known as the child-centred perspective. Child-centredness is defined as early education policies and practices that "reflect the nature of the child"[16] and are based on "observation[s] of emerging physical, social, emotional, and cognitive capabilities in children's natural activity at home and/or in early childhood settings."[17] Within the day nursery field, challenging the 'gospel' of child-centredness, is heresy, tantamount to labelling oneself as anti-child. The tying together of the two words, development and appropriate, creates a conception of practice that is both good and essential. After all, how can one be critical of something that is "appropriate" and focuses on the central "truth" of knowledge about children — their "development": "The doctrines of child-centred education ... are also distinctive for the ardour that they inspire and, as a consequence of this ardour, the indifference to any kind of objection or counter-argument that they provoke; opponents are seen at best as uncomprehending, but very likely also as malicious in intent."[18] The following discussion is an attempt to confront this dominance by setting out some of the consequences of the normative perspective.

Concept of Childhood Incompetency

In day nursery care, normative theories of development dominate how caregivers perceive the nature of children, as well as their role as caregiver. Within the normative framework, childhood is viewed as a period of life qualitatively different from adulthood. Typically the child is considered to be immature in comparison to the 'normal' adult. According to this view the child is in need of trained adult assistance in order to mature properly. Normative theories of this kind reflect, in essence, a belief that childhood is a period of incompetence.

This concept of childhood can be illustrated by the schedule of a typical day nursery. Management of time within the day nursery is entirely under the control of the caregivers, with children unable to determine their own time frame. Children's personal time, that is, when they need to eat, sleep and toilet, are superseded by the institution's timetable. The timetable is further removed from children's control by being established outside of individual nurseries by government regulations and training guidelines that provide model schedules.[19] This is not to say that day nurseries follow a rigid routine, but that high quality nurseries are expected to have a set daily schedule that reflects the needs of children as determined by normative theories of development. The concept of childhood incompetency is also reflected in the spatial organization of day nursery care. Children are viewed as incapable of deciding spatial arrangements. These decisions are made by the adult caregivers, and as with the arrangement of time, regulations and training institutions provide model guidelines. The guidelines are not based on children's views or preferences. Rather, they are framed by hypotheses as to how the space can best facilitate development, and by issues of adult control.[20]

The belief that children are incompetent pertains even when children are supposedly allowed to make independent decisions such as during 'free play' time. Free play is that time during which children are *allowed* to decide their own play activities and to engage in these largely free from adult direction. Contrary to the terminology, children are not freed from caregiver guidance during this portion of the curriculum. Instead, they are directed by the arrangement of the space, materials available, and caregiver direction as to what activities are permitted. Even in a text that proposes to "empower" children through play, the play space is not only determined by the adults, but arrived at through the application of a mathematic formula.[21] The correct formula, it is argued, will ensure that a play space offers just the right amount of complexity to satisfy the developmental play needs of the children. It is argued that an incorrect degree of complexity will require the adult "to compensate, through their own active participation or intervention, for the failure of the space to provide sufficient play opportunities."[22] Note that the child participates in this process primarily as an object to be acted upon.

The comments made by Maizie Hill, set out earlier in this book, tells us that the concept of childhood incompetency has not always been dominant. Hill recalled that at the Ottawa Day Nursery, she and other children were expected to undertake activities independent of adult decision making. Children were not given adult guidance as to what to play with or how to play, but instead were to make these decisions on their own. The perception of children as competent is not just located in the past, but can also be found in contemporary cultures where the normative perspective is not dominant. Tobin, Wu, and Davidson's research into cultural differences in day nursery caregiving found that in contrast to North American beliefs about children, Japanese caregivers viewed children as able to manage their behaviour and activities including those of play, independent of adult interference.[23]

Interpretations of Behaviours

The same lens that views children as incompetent interprets children's behaviours within the framework of progressive stages of development. From this perspective, for example, preschool children's failure to make the adult judgement that the amount of water in a container remains the same when the dimensions of the container are changed, is not explained as children making an error, or not paying attention, but by applying Piaget's theory of cognitive development that presupposes they have not yet developed particular thinking capabilities. In other word, children *cannot* provide the correct answer because they do not have the competencies of adults. Similarly, the differences between the play of two year old and five year old children, whereby two year olds are less likely to play symbolically (substituting the actual object with something else, such as pretending a rock is a frying pan) is interpreted as resulting from the two year olds' less developed intellectual abilities. From this perspective, the play activities of two year olds are not viewed as resulting from, for example, the *aesthetic pleasure* they obtain from concrete play, but from their *inability* to engage in a higher level of thinking.

The dominance of the normative perspective makes it difficult to even imagine questioning the 'truth' of these interpretations. However, different interpretations can be located historically. For instance, the Puritan interpretation of children's behaviour as a sign of God's grace. Another example: in the nineteenth century, North American children's behaviour was interpreted as a sign of their innate tendency towards evil.[24] Neither of these interpretations were based on a belief that children naturally progressed through specific stages of behaviour. Child rearing therefore was geared towards spiritual learning, in the case of the Puritans, and towards punishment during the 1800s. The comparison to other interpretations of children's behaviours demonstrates how ideas about 'good' child care are linked to meanings of childhood derived from specific social and historical contexts. Lubeck illustrates this point: "If we believe in maturation, we wait; if we believe in constructivism, we provide opportunities for children to act on the world; and, if we believe that children are 'blank slates,' we try to fill them with information through didactic instruction."[25] This helps us to understand 'developmentally appropiate caregiving practices' as social constructs rather than based upon immutable and universal laws of childhood.

Once again, ideas about play illustrates how normative interpretations of children's behaviours have been applied in day nurseries. In the early years of the nurseries, play was understood as a behaviour that children engaged in as a natural part of childhood but with no special meaning related to development or abilities. From the 1920s, children's play behaviours were reinterpreted as revealing naturally occurring stages of play development. By the 1990s, children's play was understood not just as revealing play development *per se*, but as revealing developmental abilities in all areas. For example, through play one can observe the child's development of literacy competencies. The different interpretations of play behaviours informs us that the meanings of children's play have varied over time. The tendency is to assume that such changes in interpretations are the result of the linear progress of knowledge acquisition, whereby the most recent interpretation, inevitably, is the best. The normative perspective has resulted in the abolishment of alternative ways of understanding children's play. What has been left out is an understanding of the meaning children themselves bring to their play. The omission of the child's own understandings is a serious weakness in this paradigm. In the child-centred curriculum, the child has become the central object of action, but made subordinate as an actor.

Behavioral Judgements

Integral to the normative interpretations of behaviours are the value judgements made about them; a ranking of behaviours and activities in terms of what should or should not be, of what is desirable or undesirable. Normative theories of child development judge behaviour according to a hierarchy of ability stages. From this perspective, children should move through the stages according to a specific schedule or in a specific pattern. However, normal stages of development have been mostly determined through studies of white middle class children. The behaviours and abilities of that group of children have become the standard against which other children are measured.

The value assessments inherent in a perspective that views given schedules or patterns as 'normal' make it very difficult to accept children's behaviour that is different. According to the Piagetian model, all children engage first in preoperational thinking, followed by concrete operational thinking, and then formal operational thinking. Value judgements with regard to the Piagetian stages are apparent in the care of children in typical North American day nurseries. At risk of negative judgment are children from cultures that do not priorize verbal language as a form of expression and which view the onset of language expression as part of the personality of the child (verbal language will emerge when the child needs to speak or has something to say). When such children do not speak in a 'timely' fashion, they are likely to be assessed by 'good' day nursery caregivers as being delayed in language development and therefore in need of intervention. Culturally sensitive caregivers might understand different abilities and behaviours as arising out of cultural variations in child rearing. Nevertheless, the behaviours will still be largely viewed within the dominant North American context, and as having to be modified for the child's own good. Despite the knowledge that different cultures value early speech in children differently, the dominant judgement is that all children *must* learn to express themselves according to the language patterns of the dominant society.[26]

The values inherent within beliefs about the nature of the child are also made explicit through judgements about caregiving behaviours. When play was considered an activity for children to engage in on their own, with whatever materials were available, it was not an important concern for the caregiver. It was in fact, secondary to the caregiver's role of managing the child's moral behaviour. From the 1920s, caregivers were assigned the task of observing play in order to see if it was occurring according to normative stages of play, and of ensuring the play environment was suitable for the various stages. Play was also viewed as a tool through which the child learned a variety of socially desired behaviours such as persistence, decision making, and independence. The 'good' caregiver was not to play with the child or interfere in the play as this would disrupt the naturally occurring process and remove the child's opportunities to learn the desired skills. By the 1980s, with play as a means for facilitating all areas of development, caregivers needed to observe play for opportunities to intervene directly to assist in the process. This judgement of caregiver competency can be found in assessments of nursery environments. In the *Early Childhood Environment Rating Scale* the adequacy of the play environment for the child is determined according to the following criteria:

Inadequate: *Either* little opportunity for free play *or* much of day spent in unsupervised free play. Inadequate toys, games, and equipment provided for children to use in free play.

Minimal: Some opportunity for free play, with casual supervision provided as a safety precaution. Free play not seen as an educational opportunity.

Excellent: Ample opportunity for supervised free play outdoors *and* indoors with wide range of toys, games, and equipment. Supervision used as an educational interaction.[27]

The caregiver who passively observes children's play, only intervenes on issues of safety, and who limits play materials to whatever children find in the natural environment, would be judged as inadequate by these standards. Learning about other cultural perspectives on play helps us to realize that these standards of good care are not universal. It has been reported that Japanese nursery caregivers view adult facilitation of children's play as problematic. While acknowledging that North American caregivers seem creative and fun, they worry about the impact such intervention may have on the child: "Wouldn't the children get to be too dependent on the teacher always being there to organize their play and to show them how to have fun?"[28] Within the Japanese culture, the good caregiver removes herself from children's play in order to enable children to become reliant on their own social group.

Value judgement based on the normative perspective are also problematic because of their negative influence on the provision of day nursery services. Earlier in this book, I pointed out how ideas about normal stages of social and emotional development resulted in the elimination of nursery care, until the 1980s, for children under $2\frac{1}{2}$ years. The problem with basing admission policies on the normative perspective is that this paradigm restricts understandings of children's caregiving needs to internal and individual psychological processes, rather than understanding those needs within an ecological context of the family and society. It is likely that the nurseries' attempts to restrict the ages cared for in order to provide 'good' care, resulted in many children being left without any care.

Responses to the Challenges of Diversity

Since the late 1980s, the typical approach for dealing with the cultural diversity of the children receiving child care has been the incorporation of differences into normative practice. The belief in the universal pattern of human development as it has been documented by Western child study researchers is positioned as the frame within which children's individual behaviour is interpreted.[30] The guidelines established by the National Association for Young Children posit combining universalism, individualism, and differentialism as a nonproblematic, and noncontradictory child care/early education strategy.

> Teachers can use child development knowledge to identify the range of appropriate behaviors, activities, and materials for a specific age group. This knowledge is used in conjunction with understanding about individual children's growth patterns, strengths, interests, and experiences to design the most appropriate learning environment. Although the content of the curriculum is determined by many factors such as tradition, the subject matter of the disciplines, social or cultural values, and parental desires, for the content and teaching strategies to be developmentally appropriate they must be age appropriate and individually appropriate.[30]

In their study of Canadian day care centres, Bernhard et al. found a lack of application of the above principles with regard to diversity, and concluded that resulting antagonisms between parents and child care providers could be addressed by increasing caregiver training in diversity, retaining a diverse teaching body in early childhood education, and accommodating various perspectives within the field.[31] While these are positive suggestions for improving child care, they do not challenge the normative curriculum and concomitant caregiving guidelines. Responding to diversity as if it were just another component of individualism within a universal pattern of development raises questions as to the efficacy of such approaches. How can a practice be at once universally applicable while at the same time responsive to multiple beliefs and values? Lillian Katz, a preeminent spokesperson in the child care field, proposes questioning the validity of developmental knowledge as the basis of child care practice.

If, however, the main problem among early childhood educators was simply our different conceptions of the ultimate goals of development, the links between child development knowledge and teacher preparation could simply be argued on the basis of diverse cultural expectations and preferences, rather than on whether this particular branch of knowledge is an appropriate basis for making decisions about curriculum and teaching methods.[32]

Unfortunately, Katz does not explore the question she raises beyond implying a dismissive commonsense response: if not this knowledge, then what? Katz seems unable to provide an alternative because she cannot imagine a conception of childhood or child care outside the parameters of the normative perspective; instead, she calls for more proof of the generalizability and reliability of child development knowledge.

A suggested strategy for dealing with the consequences of the normative perspective is the inclusion of a critical approach within the knowledge base of the normative curriculum.[33] Training programs as well as scholarly, professional, and popular publications would need to explicitly identify the social construction of the knowledge base, and challenge its orthodoxy. This includes identifying how the normative perspective has been used to construct and reproduce a negative bias towards maternal employment and group child care. A critical approach would also identify the limited population base upon which normative developmental schedules have been based, and how these have led to biased definitions of the abnormal, dysfunctional, and disadvantaged.

However, Bernhard (1995) warns that even presenting such a critique within a context of real life cultural practices does not necessarily lead to changed understandings. From her own attempts to do so, she found that early childhood education students were unable to seriously consider child care approaches that differed from the normative perspective.[34] An even greater danger in failing to develop meaningful alternatives for child care, is the risk of unintentionally justifying the dismantling of social provisions for day nursery services. A critique of the normative curriculum that identifies its negative consequences can be approached by persons who would use it to argue for the abolishment of child care regulations, such as requirements for caregivers to have specialized training, child-caregiver ratios, space and equipment standards, etc. Furthermore, an emphasis on the importance of culture-of-origin can be used to support arguments that parents, relatives and neighbours are better able to provide care that is based on beliefs and values of the parents, than are caregivers trained in the normative perspective. In this vision, group care conducted by trained persons would not receive public funding. A critique of the normative perspective does not suggest that there should be no specialized training for caregivers, and no day nursery regulations. Group care for children produces a situation very different from that presented by individual children in a home setting, requiring a multiplicity of caregiving skills and an environment that can accomodate the variety of demands placed upon it.

In order to be valuable to the future of child care, a critique of the normative perpective must be coupled with a different paradigm of childhood and child care, one that is grounded in an understanding of the child as a competent being who develops in a social context. If the conceptualization of childhood is understood differently from the normative perspective, then it is possible to devise a new child care curriculum. An alternative paradigm is available in the child study research of Lev Vygotsky. A psychologist in the post-revolutionary Soviet Union during the 1920s and 1930s, Vygotsky constructed a theory of human development within the Marxist framework of dialectical historical materialism. The recent English translations of Vygotsky's work has provided new insights into child development. In contrast to the normative perspective that conceptualizes development as being completed when the child demonstrates the competencies of the normal adult, Vygotsky's theory proposes that development continues as long as the individual has opportunities to engage in activities of meaning-making.[35] The Vygotskian concept of the child positions learning as leading development not as an outcome of development. Development occurs through making meaning out of activity in the social context. In designing a Vygotskian child care curriculum the temporal, spatial and interactional structures would not be organized to match age or developmental abilities, or to elicit specific learning behaviours.

Instead, these components would become the tools through which children act upon their world and thereby create meaning by engaging in self-determining activity. It is a perspective that presupposes that learning/self-activity/meaning-making, leads to new levels of development. In contrast to the developmentally appropriate approach with its inherent contradictions, grounding a child care curriculum within a Vygotskian perpective makes it possible to incorporate cultural diversity and retain at the same time the elements of humanity that are lost when the child is conceptualized as incompetent.

The Public Issue of Day Nursery Care

The expansion in numbers of day nurseries and ages of children cared for during the second half of the twentieth century as compared to the first half, is not to be taken as evidence that day nursery care came to be viewed as a 'good thing' for children or for Canadian society. In the closing years of the twentieth century, there was little evidence of political commitment to day nursery services, for either meeting the needs of children or of working parents. Therefore, theoretical revision of the childcare curriculum must be coupled with political efforts to defend and expand the public provision of day nursery services.

The first Canadian federal program directed at group child care was the provision for war time day nurseries. When that funding was withdrawn after the Second World War, federal funding was absent until the 1966 establishment of the Canadian Assistance Plan [CAP]. Initiated because of the prevailing belief in the compensatory role of early childhood education for alleviating poverty, the CAP provided federal monies to pay fifty percent of provincial day care subsidies for low-income families.[36] In April 1988, the ruling Conservative party, under the leadership of Brian Mulroney proposed the Canada Child Care Act. This was a funding proposal that if implemented would have expanded the number of licensed day nursery spaces in Canada to 200,000. Before the Bill was passed into law, the Conservatives called an election, and all bills not yet passed died, including the proposed Child Care Act. Despite a Conservative election victory, the Bill was not revived.

In 1993 the federal Liberal Party came to power promising a

national child care plan that would add $720 million over three to five years toward child care, and 150,000 new day care spaces over four years. Alas, promises made in election campaigns were once again forgotten once the party came to power. In 1996, Prime Minister Jean Chretien announced his party's abandonment of the election promise. Furthermore, federal day nursery funding available through the Canadian Assistance Plan ended in April, 1996. In place of the CAP, federal monies would be transferred to the provinces in a lump sum under a funding formula called the Canada Health and Social Transfer [CHST]. Under the new policy, provincial governments could disperse the funds as they desired amongst social programs with no guarantee or requirement that any of the monies be directed toward day nursery care. That day nurseries would likely receive less financial support under this program is evident from the direction taken in Ontario.

In 1996, under the leadership of Premier Michael Harris, the Ontario Conservative government cut funding to provincial day nurseries, resulting in a loss of 2800 subsidized spaces. Proposed changes to the Day Nurseries Act that would enable further spending reductions included increasing the number of children that could be cared for per adult in a day nursery, and lowering the training requirements of day nursery workers.[31] These changes were fueled by both a deficit-reduction program, and a belief that support for day nursery care was not the responsibility of the state.

Increased caregiver-child ratios threaten the ability of caregivers to provide for the needs of the children. While larger child-staff ratios are accepted as good practice in some cultures such as in Japanese day nursery centres, this is supported through extensive state funding and regulations. For higher child-caregiver ratios not to be seriously damaging for children, there needs to be, at the very least, the provision of physical facilities designed to accommodate larger groups of children. The typical Canadian day nursery is cramped, poorly lit and with unfavourable acoustics. Materials for children would need to be in good enough condition and quantity to support the increased demands made by greater numbers of children and reduced intervention possible when fewer caregivers are present. Caregivers need to have time away from direct contact with the children during their work day in order to plan activities and maintain records for the greater number of children for whom they are caring. Caregivers also need training in methods of supporting and encouraging a greater degree of child-child interactions than is currently expected in good Canadian child care. All of these conditions would require increased, not decreased financial support; money for more materials, more trained staff, better space. As most parents cannot afford to pay the full costs of this type of child care service, public support remains essential.

Strategies for reducing funding and standards, such as those considered by the government of Ontario, would satisfy both the demands of persons who hold the view that market principles should be applied to every aspect of life and those who view day nursery care as antagonistic to traditional family values because it enables women to engage in paid employment. An implication of provincial and federal retrenchment on supporting day nursery care is that we are moving toward eliminating day nursery care as a component of state policy, and thereby returning it to its earlier position as a private sector service. In the terminology of C. Wright Mills, day nursery care is increasingly becoming a private problem rather than a public issue.

If day care becomes a private problem, families would be forced to negotiate individually for child care services. Parents that could not afford the cost of out-of-home care would have to rely on themselves, resulting in women mainly moving out of the paid labour force in order to care for their children at home. Given current economic conditions, it is unrealistic to expect mothers to be able to leave the paid labour force to look after their own children. Therefore, group care of children will continue to be a necessary service. The withdrawal of public monies, however, will make child care harder to obtain and of poorer quality.

In a private system, parents as individuals would be wholly responsible for determining the quality of the child care purchased, including having to know about standards of care, safety issues, caregiver qualifications, and the child care curriculum. This is an unreasonable expectation. In the history of private sector day nursery care, improved quality and increased quantity have only occurred when, through the public sector, there have been financial supports for such initiatives.

The threatened removal of day nursery care from the public realm will not lead to better services. Neither will this solve the dilemmas posed by the normative perspective, especially as they pertain to issues of diversity. The history of day nursery care in Canada informs us that these problems will only get worse if we return to a reliance on philanthropy to fund and operate child care. Children and parents would once again be dependent upon the 'good will' of individual benefactors or agencies to provide a service necessary for the well-being of children and families. In the past, many children went without care because of moral judgement made by day nurseries. Caregivers would be exploited to an even greater degree than under the current system, for without training requirements they will have no basis for demanding improved wages or working conditions. There will always be a large pool of reserve, untrained, labour willing to take their places. However, the contemporary market model poses an even harsher future than a return to philanthropy. The nineteenth and early twentieth century day nursery philanthropists did not expect to recover costs of providing child care, whereas the market model is based on the expectation that when such services do not break even they will have to close down. This has already taken place in Alberta, where the University of Lethbridge closed its own child care centre because its expenses could not be met through parent fees and government funding. Unless the market model for day nursery care is defeated, we can expect more day care closures.

In presenting the history of the ideology and practice of Canadian day nursery care, and tying it to contemporary issues of state funding and regulation, this book directs attention toward a much neglected area of society, and raises a voice against the prevailing doctrine that would try to convince us that child care belongs in the private realm of families. Much has transpired over the past hundred years of day nursery care in Canada, but as this history points out, good care does not just happen. It is the outcome of many social forces and it requires both the evaluating of dominant beliefs about childhood and working actively towards creating the best possible day care policies. By making visible the relationships between ideology, policy and practice, I have shown that day nursery child care is a social issue deserving the resources necessary to meet the needs of children and their parents. The contemporary period has clearly demonstrated that hard won gains in day nursery care cannot be taken for granted. The battle for the welfare of children and families continues.

FOOTNOTES

1 Volosinov, V. N. 1973. *Marxism and the Philosophy of Language*. London: Harvard University Press, p. 78.

2 No author. 1993. "Multi-service agency enriches quality of child care" *Interaction* 7(1):20–22.

3 ODN. President's Report, 1966.

4 ODN. Annual Report, 1966.

5 ODN. Executive Director's Report, 1967.

6 ODN. Executive Director's Report, 1970.

7 WDN. "Interpretation of DNC's Service for the Budget Hearing" April 20, 1961.

8 See also Brennan, D. 1994. *The Politics of Australian Child Care: From Philanthropy to Feminism*. Cambridge, UK:Cambridge University Press.

9 WDN. Annual Report, 1967.

10 National Day Care Information Centre. 1983. *Status of Day Care in Canada. Ottawa: Health and Welfare Canada*. These figures represent the number of children that could be provided with care in both licensed day nursery centres and family day care homes.

11 ODN. Minutes, November 17, 1964.

12 ODN. Annual Report, 1965.

13 ODN. Annual Report, 1978.

14 National Day Care Information Centre. 1983. *Status of Day Care in Canada*. Ottawa: Health and Welfare Canada. These figures number of children that could be provided with care in both licensed day nursery centres and family day care homes.

15 Bredekamp, S. (Ed.), 1987. *Developmentally Appropriate Practice in Early Childhood Programs Serving Children from Birth through Age Eight*. Washington, D.C.: National Association for the Education of Young Children; Canadian Child Care Federation 1991. *National Statement on Quality*

Child Care. Ottawa: Author.

16 Darling, J. 1994. *Child-Centred Education and Its Critics.* Paul Chapman Publishing, p.3.

17 Williams, L. R. 1994. "Developmentally Appropriate Practice and Cultural Values" p. 157. In B. L. Mallory & R.S. New (Eds.), *Diversity & Developmentally Appropriate Practices: Challenges for Early Childhood Education.* NY: Teachers College Press, pp. 155–165.

18 Clark, C. 1988. "Child-Centred Education and the 'Growth' Metaphysic." *Journal of Philosophy of Education,* 22(1):75–88.

19 See for example, Canadian Child Day Care Federation, 1991.

20 See for example Esbensen, S.B. 1990. "Designing the Early Childhood Setting." In I. M. Doxey (Ed.), *Child Care and Education: Canadian Dimensions.* Scarborough, Ont.: Nelson, pp. 178-192; Prescott, E. 1981. "Relations Between Physical Setting and Adult/Child Behaviour in Day Care." In S. Kilmer (Ed.), *Advances in Early Education and Day Care,* 2. Connecticut: Jai Press: 129–158.

21 Shipley, D. 1993. *Empowering Children: Play-Based Curriculum for Lifelong Learning.* Toronto: Nelson.

22 Shipley, 1993, p. 77.

23 Tobin, J. J., Wu, D.Y.H., & Davidson, D. H. 1989. *Preschool in Three Cultures: Japan, China and the United States.* New Haven: Yale University Press.

24 Peisner, E. S. 1989. "To Spare or not to Spare the Rod: A Cultural-Historical View of Child Discipline. In J. Valsiner (Ed.), *Child Development in Cultural Context.* Toronto: Hogrefe & Huber, pp. 111–141.

25 Lubeck, S. 1996. "Deconstructing 'Child Development Knowledge' and 'Teacher Preparation." *Early Childhood Research Quarterly* 11(2):155.

26 See for example, Genishi, C., Dyson, A. H., & Fassler, R. 1992. "Language and Diversity in Early Childhood: Whose Voices are Appropriate?" In Mallory & New, pp. 250–268.

27 Harmes, T. & Clifford, R. M. 1980. *Early Childhood Environment Rating Scale.* NY: Teachers College, p. 31. Emphasis in original.

28 Quoted in Tobin, J. J., Wu, D.Y.H., & Davidson, D.H. 1991. "Forming Groups." In B. Finkelstein, A.E. Imamura & J. J. Tobin (Eds.), *Transcending Stereotypes: Discovering Japanese Culture and Education.* Yarmouth, Maine: Intercultural Press, pp. 109-118.

29 Bredekamp, 1987, p. 2.

30 Bredekamp, 1987, p. 2–3.

31 Bernhard, J. K., Lefebvre, M. L., Chud, G. & Lange, R. 1995. *Paths to Equity: Cultural, Linguistic and Racial Diversity in Canadian Early Childhood Education.* North York, Ontario: York Lane Press.

32 Katz, L. G. 1996. "Child Development Knowledge and Teacher Prepara-

tion: Confronting Assumptions." *Early Childhood Research Quarterly* *11*(2):135–146.

33 Lubeck, 1996:147–167.

34 Bernhard, J. K. 1995. "Child Development, Cultural Diversity, and the Professional Training of Early Childhood Educators." *Canadian Journal of Education 20*:415–436.

35 Vygotsky, L. S. 1978. *Mind in Society: The Development of Higher Psychological Processes*. Cambridge, Massachusetts: Harvard University Press, and Newman, F. & Holzman, L. 1993. *Lev Vygotsky: Revolutionary Scientist*. New York: Routledge.

36 For a discussion of the limitations of CAP in providing for the child care needs of low-income families, and in supporting day nursery services see Lind & Prentice, 1992.

37 "Review May Sap Day-Care Quality" *Globe and Mail*, April 8, 1996.

Join The Debate
On What Should Happen
In Canada's Schools.
You Can Still Get Your Own Copy
Of Each Of These Issues
Of Our Schools/Our Selves.

Issue #49: (Journal) Reflections on the Closure of Our Children's School ... The Music Program ... The Qualitymongers ... Let's Look Before We Leap: Standardized Testing and Special Education Students ... First Things First: Anti-Racism Education on Turtle Island ... Thinking Small a Smart Solution: Tennessee Students Reap the Benefits of Smaller Class Size ... Personal Stories, Personal Histories: Grade Eleven Students Write About Their Lives ... The Babel of Experience ... If Joe Snobelin... ... University Politics in Nicaragua ... Is Progressive Education Growing Up?

Issue #48: Teacher Activism in the 1990s edited by Susan Robertson & Harry Smaller. During the past decade, global economic restructuring has resulted in social dislocation within most advanced industrial countries. At the same time, governments at all levels have been slashing support for education, social services, health, welfare and the arts. Education has been particularly hard hit by the forces of "downsizing." Meanwhile corporations have been active in promoting "partnerships" with the public schools – both to ensure that graduates better meet *their* needs and to gain access to students as consumers.

Across Canada, as well as in other nations, teachers and their unions have been contesting and resisting both government cut-backs and private sector incursions into public education. This book offers a number of case studies of teachers' political activity in Canada, Australia, New Zealand and France. The editors as well as the contributors are educators and teacher-activists who have been observers and/or active participants in the struggle for equity and social justice in the public schools of their own communities.

Issue #47: (Journal) Ontario Teachers Try their Luck with the Class Struggle: Notes from the OSSTF Convention Floor ... The Hamilton Protest: A Photographer's Impressions ... Eduspeak: A Teacher's Guide to the Orwellian Language of the "Ministry for the Culture of Change" ...

The Butterfly vs the Bullet ... Where's the Union?: The Assualt on the
Nova Scotia Schools and the Response of the N.S. Teachers' Union ...
Hong Kong Teachers Face 1997 ... "Will you walk into my parlour?" said
the spider to the fly: Parent Participation and School Councils ... The Role
of White Parents in Overcoming Racism ... Speaking With One Voice?
But Who Benefits?: An African Canadian Parent's Response to "The Role
of White Parents in Overcoming Racism" ... What are Students Saying
about African Studies Courses in High School: A Discussion.

Double Issue #45-46: Educating African Canadians edited by
Keren S. Brathwaite & Carl E. James. Writing from their respective
locations as students, parents, teachers, counsellors, professors and
researchers, the contributors to this collection alert readers to many of the
challenges that African Canadians face today in the educational system.
The writers do not merely examine and critique the status quo in
education. They also discuss new initiatives and suggest new directions that
should improve the academic success of Black students. In addition they
offer many practical suggestions which could enhance the education not
only of African Canadian students, but of *all* students.

A common theme is the conviction that changing the current
educational system is long overdue, and that Black parents, educators and
community members must continue to engage in social action that will
lead to change in all areas of schooling. As these changes must necessarily
take into consideration the heterogeneity of the African Canadian
communities, the writers suggest diverse strategies for satisfying the needs
of African Canadians, including community-based schooling.

Issue #44: (Journal) Hyenas at the Oasis: Corporate Marketing to
Captive Students ... Madness as Resistance ... Putting Body and Soul Into
Equity Education (Part II) ... "Everybody is trying to fix me up."
Technology and the Control of Work in the Public Schools ... Education
and Technology: Virtual Studies, Digital Classroom ... "Chartering" New
Waters The Klein Revolution and the Privatization of Education in Alberta
... Aboriginal Teachers and Education Reform ... Seizing the Sociological
Moment: Citizenship Education After the Decline of History ... A Modus
Vivendi with American Kid Culture?

Issue #43: (Journal) Putting Body and Soul Into Equity Education
(Part 1) ... Quality Education and Other Myths ... In Search of a Radical
Tradition: Education Politics in France (Part 3) ... Canadian Children's
Book Creates Moral Panic in Britain ... Where to Now? New Directions

for B.C. Education ... Current Educational Reform Initiatives in New Brunswick ... Buying Minds ... Ontario's Royal Commission on Learning: Constructing a "Public Good" for the Incoming Tories? ... Education Roundup ... Ontario College for Teacher: Whose Interests Would It Serve? ... The Ideological Sell-Out of Canada.

Issue #42: A New Education Politics: Bob Rae's Legacy and the Response of the Ontario Secondary School Teachers' Federation by George Martell. Martell has written a detailed history of the Social Contract negotiations, and the pivotal role that the Ontario Secondary School Teachers' Federation (OSSTF) played in this dramatic struggle. But this book goes much further and shows how the Social Contract fits within the corporate agenda of public sector downsizing and educational reform, and how this agenda overtook the Rae government. He charts the broader government assault on the public sector and suggests how things could have been done differently. And while this history holds little comfort for all who support a strong, democratic, progressive public school system, Martell finds hope in the growing signs that teachers are beginning to stand up against the corporate agenda and fight for a different vision of education.

Double Issue #40-41: Whatever Happened To High School History? Burying the Political Memory of Youth: Ontario 1945-1995 by Bob Davis. A passionate and probing book about the decline of history as a secondary school subject. With the narrative of progress and British civilization gone, and the contemporary cult of content-free "skills" offering no basis for understanding the past, how can history teachers help today's students make sense of their world and their future?, Davis asks. Being an experienced teacher as well as a scholar and a theorist, Davis is in a unique position to pose this question and to propose new directions and new hope. A "must read" for teachers, parents and university students concerned with where our curriculum is going.

Issue #39: (Journal) Capitalism Goes to Napanee High ... Student Demonstrations in France ... Insights into Gender, Identity, Equity ... Gender Studies in the English 12 Classroom ... No Answer on Grade Nine Reading and Writing Tests ... Education Roundup ... Parents Save a School in Nova Scotia ... Cooperative/Competitive Athletics ... Reviews of Barlow, Nikiforuk, Walcom ...

Issue #38: In Defence of History: Teaching The Past And The

Meaning Of Democratic Citizenship by Ken Osborne. In the neo-conservative economic and political climate of the 1990's, history is fast becoming an endangered species. Ken Osborne, who has been teaching history for some thirty years, argues that the subject is unlike any other in the school cirriculum. How we see and interpret the world, how we understand the problems that face us on the local, national and global level, how we treat each other, our very values are largely the result of how we understand our past or fail to understand it. Besides offering a cogent argument for the importance of history, Osborne's book also provides many strategies for developing a liberating, egalitarian pedagogy, which stresses critical awareness among students, healthy scepticism about "official versions" of the past, and active student involvement in the production of socially relevant history.

Issue #37: (Journal) Globalization, NAFTA and Education ... A Year of Education Politics in France ... Teacher Morale ... View from the Classroom ... Winnipeg General Strike ... Beware of the Penguins ... What Facts, Whose Arguments? ... Going Beyond School-Based Management Before We've Even Got There ... Education Roundup ... Name One Female Inventor ... Ethics and the Corporate Classroom ... Canada/Us Border Project ... Buying In But Not Sold Out.

Issue #36: Sex In Schools edited by Susan Prentice. This anthology offers insights into how Canadian schools have sought to regulate and discipline sexuality — through sexual education classes, in teacher-student relationships, in curriculum and pedagogy, and every-day practices. The authors explore the links between sexual regulation and other forms of social organization: especially gender, sexual orientation, age, class and race.

Sex in Schools starts from the perspective that sexuality is socially constructed and is shaped by power relations. Contributors show how "normal" sexuality is created, reproduced and struggled over. From historical to contemporary examples, this anthology explores over a 150 years of Canadian education and sexual regulation.

Issue #35: (Journal) The Toronto Board Takes The Pepsi Challenge ... And Loses ... School Board NDP Failure Leads To Possible Demise ... Bombers, Kids, And Kites ... The Turkey Vulture Who Lived His Literature ... The Best and Wisest For All: A Look At Gifted Programs ... Vouchers: Will They Cure Our Schools? ... The Myth Of The "Model Minority" Rethinking The Education Of Asian Canadians ... Class Warfare: The Assault On Canada's Schools ... A Good Idea And Its Enemies Part 2: The

Best Kept Secrets Of North American Education ... Education Roundup ... A Sad Time To Be A Teacher ... Slash and Burn in Alberta Schools ... A School-leaving Literacy Test Is Not Going To Make Schools Accountable ... Teaching For Social Justice ... Neo-Conservatism In South American Education ... A Passionate Journey Into Canadian History.

Issue #34: Don't Tell Us It Can't Be Done! Alternative Classrooms In Canada And Abroad edited by Chuck Chamberlin. A remarkable collection of essays — covering a social action project in Red Deer, Alberta, a progressive school in Maryland, student governance in Sweden, the Tvind Schools of Denmark, Freinet pedagogy in France, a Piagestian school in Spain, as well as Montessori and Waldorf School programs.

Issue #33: (Journal) "Children Are Not Meant To Be Studied ..." ... Curriculum And Teaching In Canada: The Missing Centre ... More Training For What? The Canadian Labour Force Development Strategy, Saskatchewan Style ... The Regime Of Technology In Education ... Teacher Unions And Social Responsibility ... You Might Enjoy The Humble Pie At Pete's, Mr Coren ... Like Small Streams That Feed The Mississippi: Resistance In America Education ... The Lament Of A Passer-by ... Lies, Dammed Lies, And Statistics: Drop-outs, Literacy & Tests ... Education Roundup ... To Stream Or Not To Stream In Manitoba ... Getting Off The Track: Classroom Examples For An Anti-tracking Pedagogy ... Speaking Of Our World.

Issue #32: Rethinking Vocationalism edited by Rebecca Priegert Coulter and Ivor Goodson. Returns us to some of the "old questions" about education — who controls it?, and whose interests are served by it? — as they examine the "reconfiguration" of vocational education in a period of global restructuring. Other authors include Christopher J. Anstead, Jean Barman, Catherine Casey, Kari Dehli, Jane Gaskell, Madeleine R. Grumet, Nancy Jackson, Jeffry Piker and Jim Turk.

Issue #31: (Journal) The NDP and Education: What Happened In Ontario, B.C., Saskatchewan, and Manitoba? ... N.B.'s Strategy For Post-Secondary Education ... Gender Equity: A Personal Journey ... American Racism, Canadian Surrender: More Reflections On "To Kill A Mockingbird" ... A Letter From Siberia ... All The News That's Fit For Business: YNN Zeroes In On The Canadian Classroom ... Speak It! From The Heart Of Black Nova Scotia ... Educating The English.

Issue #30: Pandora's Box: Corporate Power, Free Trade and Canadian Education by John Calvert and Larry Kuehn. The authors lay bare the real story behind corporate interest in education and show, via a detailed analysis of the NAFTA text and political and economic trends throughout North America, how NAFTA is being used by Corporate Canada in their attempts to commercialize and privatize public education.

Issue #29: (Journal) Teaching Mi'kmaq: Living A Language ... TV And The Dene ... Turning A Blind Eye To Linguistic Genocide ... After 1492–1992: A Post-Colonial Supplement For The Canadian Curriculum ... The Emerging Corporate Agenda For Canadian High Schools ... A Critical Look At The Skills Mania ... Show Boat: Reflections On The Passage Of A Racist Icon ... The Ninth OISE Survey: The Public Mood In Tough Times ... A New Vision For Bilingual Education.

Issue #28: Schools And Social Justice by R.W. Connell. Throughout this broad analysis, which spans the educational systems of Europe, North America and Australia, Connell argues that the issue of social justice is fundamental to what good education is about. If the school system deals unjustly with some of its pupils, the quality of education for all of the others is degraded. He calls for "curricular justice," which opens out the perspective of the least advantaged, roots itself in a democratic context, and moves toward the creation of a more equalitarian society.

Issue #27: (Journal) NAFTA's Destruction Of Canadian Education ... The Corporate Hijacking Of Canada's Universities .... Lining Up Gender In Elementary School ... Totems and Taboos In Bilingual Education ... Teaching Outside The Mainstream ... The Nuclear Agenda In Saskatchewan's Schools ... The Anti-Racist Uses Of To Kill A Mockingbird ... New Brunswick Reading Circles ... John Dewey And American Democracy ... Surveying Canada's Teens ... Educating For Change.

Issue #26: Training For What? Labour Perspectives On Job Training by Nancy Jackson et al. In this book a number of union activists analyze the corporate training agenda in Canada and open up a labour alternative. They let us see training as a tool of political struggle in the workplace, which can contribute to skill recognition, to safe and satisfying working conditions, to career progression and to building a more democratic vision of working life.

Issue #25: (Journal) The Meaning Of Yonge Street ... What Should The NDP Do? ... New Brunswick's Plunge Into 'Excellence' ... Bargaining For Childcare ... Denmark's Efterskoles ... Reader Response And Postmodern Literacy ... Against Skills ... Slash And Burn In Nova Scotia Schools.

Issue #24: Stacking The Deck: The Streaming Of Working Class Kids In Ontario Schools by Bruce Curtis, D.W. Livingstone & Harry Smaller. This book examines the history and structure of class bias in Ontario education. It looks at both elementary and secondary schooling and proposes a new deal for working class children. The evidence is taken from the Ontario system, but the ideas and analysis can be extended to every school in Canada.

Issue #23: (Journal) Corporate Visions ... Taking On The Montreal School Commission ... Postmodern Literacy ... A Neo-Conservative Agenda In Manitoba ... Facing Up To High School Sexism ... Education In The Age Of Ecology ... An Autoworkers' Education Agenda ... Learning About Work ... The Politics Of Literacy.

Issue #22: Their Rightful Place: An Essay On Children, Families and Childcare in Canada by Loren Lind and Susan Prentice. The authors examine the complex ways we view our children in both private and public life and the care we give them inside our families and within a network of private and public childcare. They also offer an historical perspective on families and childcare in Canada and propose a strategy to develop "a free, universally accessible, publicly-funded, non-compulsory, high quality, non-profit, community-based childcare system" right across the country.

Issue #21: (Journal) The Tory Agenda ... Higher Education For Sale ... Racism and Education: Fighting Back In Nova Scotia, In A Scarborough Collegiate, In South Africa And In Victoria's Chinese Student Strike ... Saskatchewan's Neo-Conservatives ... As Neutral As My Teacher, Jesus ... "Make Work" in New Brunswick ... Teachers Politics: In Ontario And Mexico ... A Feminist Presence ... Canada's Heritage Language Programs.

Double Issue #19-20: Teaching For Democratic Citizenship by Ken Osborne. In this book Osborne extends his work in *Educating Citizens* and takes us through the world of modern pedagogies and the most recent research on effective teaching. He focuses particularly on "discovery learning," "critical pedagogy," and "feminist pedagogy" — drawing from a wide range of classroom practice — and builds on this foundation the key elements of an approach to teaching in which democratic citizenship is the core of student experience.

Issue #18: (Journal) Can The NDP Make A Difference? ... Columbus In Children's Literature ... Labour Takes On Ontario's Education Bureaucrats ... Lessons From Yukon Schools ... Vision 2000 Revisited ... Getting A Feminist Education The Hard Way ... Children In Poverty ... Reflections Of A Lesbian Teacher ... Literacy, Politics and Religion In Newfoundland ... Critiquing The National Indicators ... Student Loans In Saskatchewan ...

Issue #17: (Journal) Towards An Anti-Racist Curriculum ... Discovering Columbus ... The Baffin Writers' Project ... The Anti-Apartheid Struggle In South Africa's Schools ... What People Think About Schooling ... Children's Work ... Radical Literacy ... Getting The Gulf Into The Classroom ... Bye-Bye Minimum C Grades ... Taking Action On AIDS ...

Issue #16: (Journal) B.C.'s Privatization Of Apprenticeship ... Marketing Adult Ed In Saskatchewan ... The Future Of Ontario's CAATs ... Edmonton's Catalyst Theatre ... The Money Crisis In Nova Scotia Schools ... The Politics Of Children's Literature ... Tough Kids Out Of Control ... A Literacy Policy For Newfoundland? ... Métis Schooldays ... Capitalism And Donald Duck ... In Struggle: Ontario Elementary Teachers ...

Issue #15: Cooperative Learning And Social Change: Selected Writings Of Célestin Freinet edited and translated by David Clandfield and John Sivell. Célestin Freinet (1896-1966) pioneered an international movement for radical educational reform through cooperative learning. His pedagogy is as fresh and relevant today as it was in his own time, whether dealing with the importance of creative and useful work for children or linking schooling and community with wider issues of social justice and political action. This translation is the first to bring a broad selection of Freinet's work to an English-speaking audience.

Issue #14: (Journal) Feminism, Schools And The Union ... What's Happening in China's Schools ... N.B. Teacher Aides And The Struggle for Standards ... Barbie Dolls And Unicef ... Post-secondary Cuts In

Alberta ... CUPE-Teacher Links ... Language Control In Nova Scotia ... Pay Equity For Ontario Teachers ... Women's Struggles/Men's Responsibility ...

Double Issue #12-13: What Our High Schools Could Be: A Teacher's Reflections From The 60s To The 90s by Bob Davis. The author leads us where his experience has led him — as a teacher in a treatment centre for disturbed children, in an alternative community school, in a graduate education faculty, and for 23 years in two Metro Toronto high schools. The book ranges from powerful description to sharp analysis — from sex education to student streaming to the new skills mania.

Issue #11: (Journal) No More War Toys: The Quebec Campaign ... Labelling The Under-Fives ... Building A Socialist Curriculum ... High School Streaming in Ontario ... Growing Up Male In Nova Scotia ... New Left Academics ... Tory Cutbacks In Alberta ... More On Workers And The Rise Of Mass Schooling ... The Elementary School Ruby And How High School Turned Her Sour ...

Issue #10: Heritage Languages: The Development And Denial Of Canada's Linguistic Resources by Jim Cummins and Marcel Danesi. This book opens up the issue of teaching heritage languages in our schools to a broad audience. It provides the historical context, analyzes opposing positions, examines the rationale and research support for heritage language promotion, and looks at the future of multiculturalism and multilingualism in Canada.

Issue #9: (Journal) Rekindling Literacy In Mozambique ... Privatizing The Community Colleges ... CUPE's Educational Agenda ... High Schools & Teenage Sex ... Workers And The Rise Of Mass Schooling ... More On Nova Scotia's Children Of The State ... Grade 1 Learning ... Private School Funding ... The Globe's Attack on Media Studies ... "Consolidation" in P.E.I. ... Manitoba's High School Review ...

Issue #8: It's Our Own Knowledge: Labour, Public Education & Skills Training by Julie Davis et al. The clearest expression yet of Labour's new educational agenda for the 1990s. It begins with working-class experience in the schools and community colleges, takes issue with corporate initiatives in skills training, and proposes a program "for workers, not for bosses."

Issue #7: Claiming An Education: Feminism and Canadian Schools by Jane Gaskell, Arlene McLaren, Myra Novogrodsky. This book examines "equal opportunity," what students learn about women, what women learn about themselves and what has been accomplished by women who teach, as mothers and teachers.

Issue #6: (Journal) Labour Education And The Auto Workers ... Nova Scotia's Children Of The State ... Patrick Watson's *Democracy* ... Popular Roots Of The "New Literacy" ... Canada's Learner Centres ... Right-Wing Thinking In Education ... Fighting Sexism In Nfld. ... The Computer Bandwagon ... *Glasnost* and *Perestroika* Over Here? Funding Native Education ...

Issue #5: Building A People's Curriculum: the experience of La maîtresse d'école edited with an introduction by David Clandfield. Since 1975 this Montreal teacher collective has been producing alternative francophone curricula on labour, human rights, peace, and geo-political issues in a framework of cooperative learning. This is an anthology of their best work.

Issue #4: (Journal) Teaching The Real Stuff Of The World: Bears, History, Work Skills ... Tory Times At Sask Ed ... The NDP At The Toronto School Board ... Indian Control In Alberta Schools ... Is The Action Affirmative For Women School Board Workers ... Radwanski: The Dark Side ... More On "Whole Language" In Nova Scotia ... A Steelworker's Education ... B.C. Teachers Hang Tough ... Decoding Discrimination ...

Issue #3: (Journal) B.C. Teachers, Solidarity and Vander Zalm ... The Anti-Streaming Battle In Ontario ... The Dangers of School-Based Budgeting ... "Whole Language" In Nova Scotia ... Vancouver's Elementary Schools 1920-60 ... The Maritimes in Song and Text ... Teaching "G-Level" Kids ... The Squeeze On Alberta's Teachers ... In Winnipeg: "The Green Slime Strikes Back!" ...

Issue #2: Educating Citizens: A Democratic Socialist Agenda For Canadian Education by Ken Osborne. A coherent curriculum policy focussed on "active citizenship." Osborne takes on the issues of a "working-class curriculum" and a national "core" curriculum: what should student's know about Canada and the world at large?

Issue #1: (Journal) A Feminist Agenda For Canadian Education ... The Saskatoon Native Survival School ... School Wars: B.C., Alberta, Manitoba ... Contracting Out At The Toronto Board ... On Strike: Toronto Teachers And Saskatoon Profs ... Labour's Message In Nova Scotia Schools And Ontario ... The Free Trade Ratchet ...

Subscribe Now!

In One Year
You'll Receive
3 Journals And 3 Books.

It's Not Only
A Great Read,
It's A Great Deal.

Toll-Free Number For
Subscriptions And Book Orders
1-800-565-1975.

Subscribe & Save

Please enter my subscription for 6 issues of OUR SCHOOLS/OUR SELVES starting with issue number_____. Please check one:

INDIVIDUAL

_____ Regular rate	$38.00
_____ Student/Unemployed/	
Pensioner rate	$32.00
_____ Outside Canada	Cdn $50.00

ORGANIZATION

_____ In Canada	$50.00
_____ Outside Canada	Cdn $60.00

SUSTAINING

_____ $100   _____ $200   Other $_____

OR send me issue number(s) _____ at $9.00 per single and $16.00 per double issue

To subscribe please phone our toll-free number at 1-800-565-1975 or mail form to *Our Schools/Our Selves*, 5502 Atlantic Street, Halifax, NS B3H 9Z9

Name_____

Address_____

City _____ Prov _____ Code _____

Occupation _____

☐ Cheque enclosed   ☐ VISA/Mastercard

Card No._____ Expiry Date _____

Signature _____

- -

Pass to a Friend

Please enter my subscription for 6 issues of OUR SCHOOLS/OUR SELVES starting with issue number_____. Please check one:

INDIVIDUAL

_____ Regular rate	$38.00
_____ Student/Unemployed/	
Pensioner rate	$32.00
_____ Outside Canada	Cdn $50.00

ORGANIZATION

_____ In Canada	$50.00
_____ Outside Canada	Cdn $60.00

SUSTAINING

_____ $100   _____ $200   Other $_____

OR send me issue number(s) _____ at $9.00 per single and $16.00 per double issue

To subscribe please phone our toll-free number at 1-800-565-1975 or mail form to *Our Schools/Our Selves*, 5502 Atlantic Street, Halifax, NS B3H 9Z9

Name_____

Address_____

City _____ Prov _____ Code _____

Occupation _____

☐ Cheque enclosed   ☐ VISA/Mastercard

Card No._____ Expiry Date _____

Signature _____

The Our Schools/Our Selves Series

James Lorimer & Company is now distributing and marketing the Our Schools/Our Selves book series. New titles will be published as series titles. The backlist of titles is now available to the trade through James Lorimer & Company.
Our Schools/Our Selves subscribers will continue to receive copies of these titles as they are published, as part of their *OS/OS* subscription.
Libraries and bookstores can order *Our Schools/ Our Selves* from James Lorimer & Company through its distributor:

Formac Distributing Limited
5502 Atlantic Street
Halifax B3H 1G4
Toll free order line 1-800-565-1975
Fax orders (902) 425-0166

In the U.S.:
Formac Distributing Limited
121 Mount Vernon Street
Boston MA 02108
1-800-565-1975

Contact the order desk to be sure to receive your copy of the 1996 Lorimer university catalogue